MODERN POETS
Three

Modern Poets

⟍THREE⟍

edited by

JIM HUNTER

Senior English Master
Bristol Grammar School

FABER AND FABER
24 Russell Square
London

First published in 1968
by Faber and Faber Limited
24 Russell Square London WC1
Printed in Great Britain by
Latimer Trend & Co Ltd Plymouth
All rights reserved

SBN (hard bound edition) 571 08860 0
SBN (paper bound edition) 571 08861 9

CONTENTS

7

INTRODUCTION

This book is one of a series of four, which I really see as a single collection. In these four volumes are printed selections from twenty-two modern poets whose language is English. I have tried to pick the poets that it would be most useful to have in such a collection, but it would be rash to assert that these are the best poets of their time. Simpler to say: here are some recent poets that deserve our attention. Choosing them was not easy. The omission I most regret is that of the Scots poet Hugh Mac-Diarmid, a controversial figure but one of the most interesting this century: it was felt that the Lallans in which his best work is written would stand too much in the way of readers of this anthology.

Poets are printed here in order of their date of birth. This seemed sounder than attempting to group them according to patterns which not all readers might accept.

More space has been given to some poets than to others. This should not be seen as crude value-judgement—some poets (e.g. D. H. Lawrence) are more discursive than others (e.g. Wallace Stevens). It is true, of course, that where a poet is given an unusual amount of space this is because he seems to me to offer a wide range of distinguished writing, which should be represented as fairly as possible.

There is still more apparent unfairness in the amount of notes supplied for different poets. But this, too, is not in itself a comment on the merit or interest of the poets:

some modern writers are straightforward, others are difficult. The space for notes in these books has been kept down, in order to print plenty of poetry; and the notes have had to be confined largely to necessary explanation of difficulties, though I have tried to suggest some critical approaches, and have asked one or two questions to keep the reader awake.

In writing the notes I have, of course, drawn freely on various critical works, biographies and commentaries. The notes are intended to be simple and minimal; and anyone seriously studying the poets will need to read about their work and lives for himself. In choosing poets and poems, and in writing the notes, I have been helped by conversation with a number of friends, and in particular by Frank Beecroft, Bill Haxworth, Fred Inglis, and Andor Gomme.

W. H. Auden

W. H. Auden was born in York in 1907 and educated at a public school before going up to Oxford, where he was lionized and where he rapidly became the central figure in a brilliant group of young writers and would-be politicians. Among his friends and associates were Louis MacNeice, Cecil Day Lewis and Stephen Spender, and, from Cambridge, the novelist Christopher Isherwood. Spender's autobiography *World within World* gives a fascinating account of Auden at Oxford. Auden's first book of poems was published in 1930. He was a schoolmaster for a while, wrote verse plays with Isherwood, film scripts, and other commissioned work, and became the most famous young poet in England before the Second World War. He emigrated to the United States in 1939; and has continued to publish poetry at intervals.

Auden was perhaps unfortunate in acquiring when very young the label of 'major poet'. Most people today feel that he is one of the more important figures in twentieth-century English literature, but, considering that they accept this, they are strangely reserved in their praise. It is probably fair to say that Auden's technical skill and ease are usually more impressive than what he actually says; though he is—particularly in his earlier work—very much a poet of 'ideas'. He is master of the verse-forms of the past, and of pastiche of ancient love-poets or satirists; and there is a recurrent sense of the absurd, which makes him a good writer of light verse. (As joint-editor of an excellent school anthology *The Poet's Tongue*, which readers may know, he did much to put gaiety and energy back into English teaching in our schools.) But Auden is primarily a serious poet, and should be judged as such.

13

He stands for humanity, against the anonymity of modern society; for humane stoicism, against the bestiality of modern warfare and political persecution. He is quite clearly a poet of warm intentions, occasionally over-earnest in his youth, dry and self-critical in middle age. In the 1930's his thinking and poetry lean towards Communism; in the 1950's, towards High-Church Christianity; in both cases, human decency and kindness are perhaps his strongest motives. But for all the warm intentions, Auden's poetry seems lacking in close personal involvement. There are many generalizations about humanity, few specific instances: and the poet himself remains a vague personality, not a distinct individual in contact with other individuals. Auden writes once or twice sardonically about the superiority of the novelist to the poet; how seriously this is meant is doubtful, but it is true that his own poetry seems unusually lacking in the realization of people, places and events. Landscapes and incidents—even people—in Auden are repeatedly allegorical; one eventually begins to long for 'the thing itself'.

The selection printed here is affected by Auden's unceasing revision and suppression of his past work. One poem in particular I wanted to include: the very famous and moving IST SEPTEMBER 1939, which many readers find Auden's most impressive single poem; but permission to reprint it was refused. It is also omitted from the *Collected Shorter Poems 1927–1957*; but one can still find it in earlier Auden collections and many anthologies.

Approach Auden through his verse, whether in obviously 'musical' exercises such as ON THIS ISLAND or in the intensely serious IN MEMORY OF W. B. YEATS. Variety and precision, twentieth-century ease and a classical sense of tradition, combine most impressively in Auden: here it is that he carries, most persuasively, the ring of greatness.

14

On This Island

Look, stranger, on this island now
The leaping light for your delight discovers,
Stand stable here
And silent be,
That through the channels of the ear
May wander like a river
The swaying sound of the sea.

Here at the small field's ending pause
Where the chalk wall falls to the foam and its
    tall ledges
Oppose the pluck
And knock of the tide,
And the shingle scrambles after the suck-
-ing surf,
And the gull lodges
A moment on its sheer side.

Far off like floating seeds the ships
Diverge on urgent voluntary errands,
And the full view
Indeed may enter
And move in memory as now these clouds do,
That pass the harbour mirror
And all the summer through the water saunter.

Lullaby

Lay your sleeping head, my love,
Human on my faithless arm;
Time and fevers burn away
Individual beauty from
Thoughtful children, and the grave
Proves the child ephemeral:
But in my arms till break of day
Let the living creature lie,
Mortal, guilty, but to me
The entirely beautiful.

Soul and body have no bounds:
To lovers as they lie upon
Her tolerant enchanted slope
In their ordinary swoon,
Grave the vision Venus sends
Of supernatural sympathy,
Universal love and hope;
While an abstract insight wakes
Among the glaciers and the rocks
The hermit's sensual ecstasy.

Certainty, fidelity
On the stroke of midnight pass
Like vibrations of a bell
And fashionable madmen raise
Their pedantic boring cry:
Every farthing of the cost,
All the dreaded cards foretell,
Shall be paid, but from this night
Not a whisper, not a thought,
Not a kiss nor look be lost.

Beauty, midnight, vision dies:
Let the winds of dawn that blow
Softly round your dreaming head
Such a day of sweetness show
Eye and knocking heart may bless,
Find the mortal world enough;
Noons of dryness see you fed
By the involuntary powers,
Nights of insult let you pass
Watched by every human love.

'Fish in the unruffled lakes...'

Fish in the unruffled lakes
The swarming colours wear,
Swans in the winter air
A white perfection have,
And the great lion walks
Through his innocent grove;
Lion, fish, and swan
Act, and are gone
Upon Time's toppling wave.

We till shadowed days are done,
We must weep and sing
Duty's conscious wrong,
The Devil in the clock,
The Goodness carefully worn
For atonement or for luck;
We must lose our loves,
On each beast and bird that moves
Turn an envious look.

Sighs for folly said and done
Twist our narrow days;
But I must bless, I must praise
That you, my swan, who have
All gifts that to the swan
Impulsive Nature gave,
The majesty and pride,
Last night should add
Your voluntary love.

from *Letter to Lord Byron*

The North, though, never was your cup of tea;
  'Moral' you thought it so you kept away.
And what I'm sure you're wanting now from me
  Is news about the England of the day.
    What sort of things La Jeunesse do and say.   5
Is Brighton still as proud of her pavilion,
And is it safe for girls to travel pillion?

I'll clear my throat and take a Rover's breath
  And skip a century of hope and sin—
For far too much has happened since your death.   10
  Crying went out and the cold bath came in,
  With drains, bananas, bicycles, and tin,
And Europe saw from Ireland to Albania
The Gothic Revival and the Railway Mania.

We're entering now the Eotechnic phase   15
  Thanks to the Grid and all those new alloys;
That is, at least, what Lewis Mumford says.
  A world of Aertex underwear for boys,
  Huge plate-glass windows, walls absorbing noise,
Where the smoke nuisance is utterly abated   20
And all the furniture is chromium-plated.

Well, you might think so if you went to Surrey
  And stayed for week-ends with the well-to-do,
Your car too fast, too personal your worry
  To look too closely at the wheeling view.   25
  But in the north it simply isn't true.
To those who live in Warrington or Wigan,
It's not a white lie, it's a whacking big 'un.

There on the old historic battlefield,
30   The cold ferocity of human wills,
The scars of struggle are as yet unhealed;
    Slattern the tenements on sombre hills,
    And gaunt in valleys the square-windowed mills
That, since the Georgian house, in my conjecture
35   Remain our finest native architecture.

On economic, health or moral grounds,
    It hasn't got the least excuse to show;
No more than chamber pots or otter hounds:
    But let me say before it has to go,
40   It's the most lovely country that I know;
Clearer than Scafell Pike, my heart has stamped on
The view from Birmingham to Wolverhampton.

Long, long ago, when I was only four,
    Going towards my grandmother, the line
45   Passed through a coal-field. From the corridor
    I watched it pass with envy, thought 'How fine!
    Oh how I wish that situation mine.'
Tramlines and slagheaps, pieces of machinery,
That was, and still is, my ideal scenery.

50   Hail to the New World! Hail to those who'll love
    Its antiseptic objects, feel at home.
Lovers will gaze at an electric stove,
    Another poésie de départ come
    Centred round bus-stops or the aerodrome.
55   But give me still, to stir imagination
The chiaroscuro of the railway station.

Preserve me from the Shape of Things to Be;
   The high-grade posters at the public meeting,
The influence of Art on Industry,
   The cinemas with perfect taste in seating;   60
   Preserve me, above all, from central heating.
It may be D. H. Lawrence hocus-pocus,
But I prefer a room that's got a focus.

But you want facts, not sighs. I'll do my best
   To give a few; you can't expect them all.   65
To start with, on the whole we're better dressed;
   For chic the difference today is small
   Of barmaid from my lady at the Hall.
It's sad to spoil this democratic vision
With millions suffering from malnutrition.   70

Again, our age is highly educated;
   There is no lie our children cannot read,
And as MacDonald might so well have stated
   We're growing up and up and up indeed.
   Advertisements can teach us all we need;   75
And death is better, as the millions know,
Than dandruff, night-starvation, or B.O.

We've always had a penchant for field sports,
   But what do you think has grown up in our towns?
A passion for the open air and shorts;   80
   The sun is one of our emotive nouns.
   Go down by chara' to the Sussex Downs,
Watch the manœuvres of the week-end hikers
Massed on parade with Kodaks or with Leicas.

85   These movements signify our age-long rule
       Of insularity has lost its powers;
    The cult of salads and the swimming pool
       Comes from a climate sunnier than ours,
       And lands which never heard of licensed hours.
90   The south of England before very long
    Will look no different from the Continong.

    You lived and moved among the best society
       And so could introduce your hero to it
    Without the slightest tremor of anxiety;
95   Because he was your hero and you knew it,
    He'd know instinctively what's done, and do it.
    He'd find our day more difficult than yours
    For Industry has mixed the social drawers.

    We've grown, you see, a lot more democratic,
100   And Fortune's ladder is for all to climb;
    Carnegie on this point was most emphatic.
       A humble grandfather is not a crime,
       At least, if father made enough in time!
    Today, thank God, we've got no snobbish feeling
105   Against the more efficient modes of stealing.

    The porter at the Carlton is my brother,
       He'll wish me a good evening if I pay,
    For tips and men are equal to each other.
       I'm sure that *Vogue* would be the first to say
110   Que le Beau Monde is socialist today;
    And many a bandit, not so gently born
    Kills vermin every winter with the Quorn.

*   *   *

Now for the spirit of the people. Here
   I know I'm treading on more dangerous ground:
I know there're many changes in the air,   115
   But know my data too slight to be sound.
   I know, too, I'm inviting the renowned
Retort of all who love the Status Quo:
'You can't change human nature, don't you know!'

We've still, it's true, the same shape and appearance,   120
   We haven't changed the way that kissing's done;
The average man still hates all interference,
   Is just as proud still of his new-born son:
   Still, like a hen, he likes his private run,
Scratches for self-esteem, and slyly pecks   125
A good deal in the neighbourhood of sex.

But he's another man in many ways:
   Ask the cartoonist first, for he knows best.
Where is the John Bull of the good old days,
   The swaggering bully with the clumsy jest?   130
   His meaty neck has long been laid to rest,
His acres of self-confidence for sale;
He passed away at Ypres and Passchendaele.

Turn to the work of Disney or of Strube;
   There stands our hero in his threadbare seams;   135
The bowler hat who strap-hangs in the tube,
   And kicks the tyrant only in his dreams,
   Trading on pathos, dreading all extremes;
The little Mickey with the hidden grudge;
Which is the better, I leave you to judge.   140

Begot on Hire-Purchase by Insurance,
   Forms at his christening worshipped and adored;
A season ticket schooled him in endurance,
   A tax collector and a waterboard
145   Admonished him. In boyhood he was awed
By a matric, and complex apparatuses
Keep his heart conscious of Divine Afflatuses.

'I am like you,' he says, 'and you, and you,
   I love my life, I love the home-fires, have
150   To keep them burning. Heroes never do.
      Heroes are sent by ogres to the grave.
      I may not be courageous, but I save.
I am the one who somehow turns the corner,
I may perhaps be fortunate Jack Horner. . . .'

In Memory of W. B. Yeats

(d. Jan. 1939)

I

He disappeared in the dead of winter:
The brooks were frozen, the airports deserted,
And snow disfigured the public statues;
The mercury sank in the mouth of the dying day.
What instruments we have agree   5
The day of his death was a dark cold day.

Far from his illness
The wolves ran on through the evergreen forests,
The peasant river was untempted by the fashionable
     quays;
By mourning tongues   10
The death of the poet was kept from his poems.

But for him it was his last afternoon as himself,
An afternoon of nurses and rumours;
The provinces of his body revolted,
The squares of his mind were empty,   15
Silence invaded the suburbs,
The current of his feeling failed; he became his
     admirers.

Now he is scattered among a hundred cities
And wholly given over to unfamiliar affections,
To find his happiness in another kind of wood   20
And be punished under a foreign code of conscience.
The words of a dead man
Are modified in the guts of the living.

But in the importance and noise of to-morrow
When the brokers are roaring like beasts on the floor
of the Bourse,
And the poor have the sufferings to which they are
fairly accustomed,
And each in the cell of himself is almost convinced of his
freedom,
A few thousand will think of this day
As one thinks of a day when one did something slightly
unusual.
What instruments we have agree
The day of his death was a dark cold day.

II

You were silly like us; your gift survived it all:
The parish of rich women, physical decay,
Yourself. Mad Ireland hurt you into poetry.
Now Ireland has her madness and her weather still,
For poetry makes nothing happen: it survives
In the valley of its making where executives

Would never want to tamper, flows on south
From ranches of isolation and the busy griefs,
Raw towns that we believe and die in; it survives,
A way of happening, a mouth.

III

Earth, receive an honoured guest:
William Yeats is laid to rest.
Let the Irish vessel lie
Emptied of its poetry.   45

In the nightmare of the dark
All the dogs of Europe bark,
And the living nations wait,
Each sequestered in its hate;

Intellectual disgrace   50
Stares from every human face,
And the seas of pity lie
Locked and frozen in each eye.

Follow, poet, follow right
To the bottom of the night,   55
With your unconstraining voice
Still persuade us to rejoice;

With the farming of a verse
Make a vineyard of the curse,
Sing of human unsuccess   60
In a rapture of distress;

In the deserts of the heart
Let the healing fountain start,
In the prison of his days
Teach the free man how to praise.   65

Like a Vocation

Not as that dream Napoleon, rumour's dread and centre,
Before whose riding all the crowds divide,
Who dedicates a column and withdraws,
Not as that general favourite and breezy visitor
To whom the weather and the ruins mean so much,
Nor as any of those who always will be welcome,
As luck or history or fun,
Do not enter like that: all these depart.

Claim, certainly, the stranger's right to pleasure:
Ambassadors will surely entertain you
With knowledge of operas and men,
Bankers will ask for your opinion
And the heiress' cheek lean ever so slightly towards you,
The mountains and the shopkeepers accept you
And all your walks be free.

But politeness and freedom are never enough,
Not for a life. They lead
Up to a bed that only looks like marriage;
Even the disciplined and distant admiration
For thousands who obviously want nothing
Becomes just a dowdy illness. These have their moderate
    success;
They exist in the vanishing hour.

But somewhere always, nowhere particularly unusual,
Almost anywhere in the landscape of water and houses,
His crying competing unsuccessfully with the cry
Of the traffic or the birds, is always standing

The one who needs you, that terrified
Imaginative child who only knows you
As what the uncles call a lie,
But knows he has to be the future and that only
The meek inherit the earth, and is neither
Charming, successful, nor a crowd;
Alone among the noise and policies of summer
His weeping climbs towards your life like a vocation.

The Model

Generally, reading palms or handwriting or faces
    Is a job of translation, since the kind
        Gentleman often is
    A seducer, the frowning schoolgirl may
        Be dying to be asked to stay;
But the body of this old lady exactly indicates her mind.

Rorschach or Binet could not add to what a fool can see
    From the plain fact that she is alive and well;
        For when one is eighty
    Even a teeny-weeny bit of greed
        Makes one very ill indeed,
And a touch of despair is instantaneously fatal:

Whether the town once drank bubbly out of her shoes or
        whether
    She was a governess with a good name
        In Church circles, if her
    Husband spoiled her or if she lost her son,
        Is by this time all one.
She survived her true condition; she forgave; she
        became.

So the painter may please himself; give her an English
        park,
    Rice-fields in China, or a slum tenement;
        Make the sky light or dark;
    Put green plush behind her or a red brick wall.
        She will compose them all,
Centring the eye on their essential human element.

In Transit

Let out where two fears intersect, a point selected
    Jointly by general staffs and engineers,
In a wet land, facing rough oceans, never invaded
    By Caesars or a cartesian doubt, I stand,
Pale, half asleep, inhaling its new fresh air that smells
    So strongly of soil and grass, of toil and gender,
But not for long: a professional friend is at hand
    Who smiling leads us indoors; we follow in file,

Obeying that fond peremptory tone reserved for those
    Nervously sick and children one cannot trust,
Who might be tempted by ponds or learn some disgusting
    Trick from a ragamuffin. Through modern panes
I admire a limestone hill I have no permission to climb
    And the pearly clouds of a sunset that seems
Oddly early to me: maybe an ambitious lad stares back,
    Dreaming of elsewhere and our godlike freedom.

Somewhere are places where we have really been, dear
      spaces
    Of our deeds and faces, scenes we remember
As unchanging because there we changed, where shops
      have names,
    Dogs bark in the dark at a stranger's footfall
And crops grow ripe and cattle fatten under the kind
    Protection of a godling or goddessling
Whose affection has been assigned them, to heed their
      needs and
    Plead in heaven the special case of their place.

Somewhere, too, unique for each, his frontier dividing
    Past from future, reached and crossed without
        warning:
That bridge where an ageing destroyer takes his last
        salute,
    In his rear all rivals fawning, in cages
Or dead, ahead a field of wrath; and that narrow pass
        where,
    Late from a sullen childhood, a fresh creator
Yields, glowing, to a boyish rapture, wild gothic peaks
        above him,
    Below, Italian sunshine, Italian flesh.

But here we are nowhere, unrelated to day or to Mother
    Earth in love or in hate; our occupation
Leaves no trace on this place or each other who do not
    Meet in its mere enclosure but are exposed
As objects for speculation, aggressive creatures
    On their way to their prey but now quite docile,
Told to wait and controlled by a voice that from time to
        time calls
    Some class of souls to foregather at the gate.

It calls me again to our plane and soon we are floating
        above
    A possessed congested surface, a world; down there
Motives and natural processes are stirred by spring
    And wrongs and graves grow greenly; slaves in
        quarries
Against their wills feel the will to live renewed by the
        song
    Of a loose bird, maculate cities are spared
Through the prayers of illiterate saints, and an ancient
    Feud re-opens with the debacle of a river.

First Things First

Woken, I lay in the arms of my own warmth and listened
To a storm enjoying its storminess in the winter dark
Till my ear, as it can when half-asleep or half-sober,
Set to work to unscramble that interjectory uproar,
Construing its airy vowels and watery consonants
Into a love-speech indicative of a Proper Name.

Scarcely the tongue I should have chosen, yet, as well
As harshness and clumsiness would allow, it spoke in
    your praise,
Kenning you a god-child of the Moon and the West Wind
With power to tame both real and imaginary monsters,
Likening your poise of being to an upland county,
Here green on purpose, there pure blue for luck.

Loud though it was, alone as it certainly found me,
It reconstructed a day of peculiar silence
When a sneeze could be heard a mile off, and had me
    walking
On a headland of lava beside you, the occasion as ageless
As the stare of any rose, your presence exactly
So once, so valuable, so very now.

This, moreover, at an hour when only too often
A smirking devil annoys me in beautiful English,
Predicting a world where every sacred location
Is a sand-buried site all cultured Texans do,
Misinformed and thoroughly fleeced by their guides,
And gentle hearts are extinct like Hegelian Bishops.

Grateful, I slept till a morning that would not say
How much it believed of what I said the storm had said
But quietly drew my attention to what had been done
—So many cubic metres the more in my cistern
Against a leonine summer—, putting first things first:
Thousands have lived without love, not one without
water.

Notes

ON THIS ISLAND

This is a good painting, and enjoyable as that; but even more
it is a sound-picture, and a pattern of sound in its own right.
Rhyme, half-rhyme, assonance, alliteration abound in the
poem, but they are used delicately, so that it is attractively
speakable. It is hard to think of anything in English poetry
quite like the dreamy sliding-together of words in the last two
lines.

LULLABY

A song-like poem in a classic and popular manner, but neither
cheap nor stale. A personal tenderness pervades this poem
which one sometimes misses in Auden's larger gestures.

The first verse treats a traditional theme: mortal beauty
passes, but at least this night is ours. The second develops an
equally familiar idea: 'soul and body have no bounds'—phy-
sical lovers experience the loftiest spiritual revelations, and
abstract thought may awaken in a hermit a bodily excitement.
The third verse speaks of the dangers and hostilities of the
world outside: the lovers will have to face the consequences
of their present happiness, but the happiness will be remem-
bered, will not be lost. The first line of the last verse refers
back to the previous three: this verse is a prayer for the
welfare of the beloved.

'FISH IN THE UNRUFFLED LAKES . . .'

A twentieth-century love-song of great delicacy and warmth.
It is important to see that the argument of the whole poem
builds up to the last two lines.

from LETTER TO LORD BYRON

This long poem was written in response to a Faber commission which helped Auden to visit Iceland in 1936 with Louis MacNeice: the resulting book, to which both contributed, is called *Letters from Iceland*.

George Gordon, Lord Byron, is usually and understandably linked with his great Romantic contemporaries, Keats, Shelley and Wordsworth; but arguably his best (and certainly his most interesting) work is in his satirical poems, of which the mock-epic *Don Juan* is the most important. Auden here uses a stanza similar though not identical to that of *Don Juan* and brilliantly imitates Byron's chatty, casual tone and impudent rhymes. His poem is a light-hearted but clear-eyed account of Britain in the mid-1930's, and of Auden's own life and concerns. It represents at its best Auden's liking for foolery, and—as is quickly evident in the extract printed here—by no means lacks seriousness.

17. *Lewis Mumford*: famous writer on cities and living habits of the future.

56. *chiaroscuro*: light and shade effect.

62. Lawrence also disliked modern synthetic creations; Auden (not a fervent admirer of Lawrence's work) is embarrassed to find himself on Lawrence's side for once.

73. *MacDonald*: Ramsay MacDonald, first Labour Prime Minister. One of his more notorious remarks is parodied in the following line.

93. *your hero*: Don Juan.

101. *Carnegie*: Dale Carnegie.

109. *Vogue*: London high-society fashion magazine.

110. *le Beau Monde*: the world of fashion.

112. *the Quorn*: a Hunt.

133. *Ypres and Passchendaele*: battlefields of the First World War.

134. *Disney*: Hollywood cartoon-film-maker. *Strube*: cartoonist of the 20's and 30's.

146. *matric*: equivalent of today's G.C.E.

147. *Divine Afflatuses*: literally, divine inspirations. Auden *may* be referring to such mechanical aids to art as the cinema and gramophone.

154. One of the excellences of LETTER TO LORD BYRON is its continuity: it is not easy to know where to stop one's extract. Here it is the editor's fault, not Auden's, that the passage ends on the cheerfully awful rhyme about Jack Horner. . . .

IN MEMORY OF W. B. YEATS

Yeats (1865–1939) was one of the greatest twentieth-century poets (he is substantially represented in Volume One of the present series). Auden was growing up just as Yeats published his best work, and he is at times clearly indebted to Yeats, for example in 1ST SEPTEMBER 1939. This poem in tribute to Yeats is one of the most consistently dignified and powerful Auden has written.

Yeats was, amongst other things, a master of epigram—the summing-up of a complex idea in a brilliant brief statement—and in this poem Auden shows something of the same ability, for example in lines 17 or 27.

Auden tends frequently towards allegory; here lines 1–6 are not to be taken merely as observations about the month of the year. The year itself, 1939, is relevant (compare Mac-Neice's AUTUMN JOURNAL or Auden's 1ST SEPTEMBER 1939, and lines 46–54 here). Why are the public statues mentioned (line 3)?

The Bourse (line 25) is the Paris Stock Exchange.

33. *the parish of rich women*: Yeats's genius survived what many would have seen as the hazard of association with the Irish aristocracy, lady patrons of the arts and lady politicians. *physical decay*: is one of the difficult themes which Yeats's later poetry handles superbly.

34. Irish nationalism, and the follies and excellences of the Irish people, are often treated in Yeats's poems.

39–40. To describe what he sees as the unsophisticated, pioneer, impractical art of poetry, Auden uses the image of

37

American rather than European landscape. He had recently settled in the United States.

The verse of section III has suggestions of that of William Blake, a writer Yeats himself fiercely admired and tried to imitate.

49. *sequestered*: cut off from others.

59–65. Much of Yeats's greatest poetry is a record of dissatisfaction and failure; but by its self-criticism and aspiration it has a positive force. Auden wishes us all to learn the same art.

LIKE A VOCATION

The poet addresses someone, presumably the reader; and seems to be offering us advice on what to try to make of our lives. The poem asserts the importance of a fundamentally humane, unglamorous life, lived for the sake of another person; and rejects as, in comparison, wrong or at best inadequate all conventional notions of the noble life. The last section of the poem—the easiest to follow, and the most urgent—is characteristic of a quality which distinguishes Auden's best verse: intense seriousness and dignity achieved in apparently casual, colloquial, unrhetorical verse.

THE MODEL

The face and bearing of the old lady speak of her human decency and goodness, even though one may not know from what social class she comes or what have been the conditions of her life. In such faces an 'essential human element' speaks out.

Rorschach and *Binet*: devisers of psychological tests.

IN TRANSIT

This, and FIRST THINGS FIRST, illustrate Auden's more serious post-war mood (he has also written a good deal of frivolous verse of characteristic wit and delicacy). Rhyme tends to be used less, but the lines are weighty and disciplined (and there is much *internal* rhyme in IN TRANSIT).

The poet has to change planes, to wait between two journeys both of which frighten him, at an airport in a strange country. The experience unsettles his confidence in the reality of his own situation. Auden's tendency to allegorize landscape emerges again: see the fourth verse (which considers the scenes which are especially significant to each person, as contrasted with the airport which means nothing to them), or the end of the fifth verse (souls being called to a gate). *Cartesian* in the first verse probably here means 'philosophical'; *maculate* in the last verse means 'flawed, corrupt'.

FIRST THINGS FIRST
Wakening alone in the night storm, the poet remembers vividly a loved one and a place (sacred in his memory) which they visited together. The depressed fourth verse increases the poignancy of this recollection by commenting that sacred places tend more and more to be abominably touristified, and that perhaps the 'gentle hearts' that made such places sacred are extinct. When he wakes again to daylight the sharp memory has passed, and he concentrates on the humdrum reality: the storm brought him water, which is in one way more important than love. (But only in one way: regret remains the main statement of the poem.)

Louis MacNeice

Louis MacNeice was born in 1907 and spent his early child-
hood in Ireland, and although he spent most of his adult life
in England he often seemed something of an exile. He was a
university teacher of classics during the 1930's, and was a
friend of and collaborator with W. H. Auden, with whom he
had been at Oxford. In the 1940's he worked at the B.B.C.,
writing and producing radio plays of a high standard. He
died in 1965.

MacNeice's fate for many years was to be regarded as one
of 'the Thirties poets': therefore political and dated. It is true
that his long poem AUTUMN JOURNAL expresses the feelings
of a London-dweller at a crucial moment in modern European
history; and that he is at his best in painting the twentieth-
century city landscape. But he is not a political writer, and is
in no way 'dated'. MacNeice had the most traditional kind of
lyric talent of all the poets who became famous during the
1930's. His songs are more genuinely songs than those of
Auden: the Irish lilt is there unobtrusively in most of his
poems—not, usually, a lilt of joy, but of a desperate amuse-
ment in the face of a discouraging life. He is a poet of
humanity, mood and moment, not of abstract or philosophical
concerns. MacNeice's poetry is a repeated invitation to the
reader to 'join hands', to create some kind of human contact
to keep away 'the wolves of water/Who howl along our coast.'
Time and again he speaks for the reasonable sensitive man of
our times, with taste and restraint—and with the dash of
fancy and verbal music which makes his statements poetry.

Wolves

I do not want to be reflective any more
Envying and defying unreflective things
Finding pathos in dogs and undeveloped handwriting
And young girls doing their hair and all the castles of sand
Flushed, by the children's bedtime, level with the shore.

The tide comes in and goes out again, I do not want
To be always stressing either its flux or its permanence,
I do not want to be a tragic or philosophic chorus
But to keep my eye only on the nearer future
And after that let the sea flow over us.

Come then, all of you, come closer, form a circle
Join hands and make believe that joined
Hands will keep away the wolves of water
Who howl along our coast. And be it assumed
That no one hears them among the talk and laughter.

Train to Dublin

Our half-thought thoughts divide in sifted wisps
Against the basic facts repatterned without pause,
I can no more gather my mind up in my fist
Than the shadow of the smoke of this train upon the
    grass—
This is the way that animals' lives pass.   5

The train's rhythm never relents, the telegraph posts
Go striding backwards like the legs of time to where
In a Georgian house you turn at the carpet's edge
Turning a sentence while, outside my window here,
10   The smoke makes broken queries in the air.

The train keeps moving and the rain holds off,
I count the buttons on the seat, I hear a shell
Held hollow to the ear, the mere
Reiteration of integers, the bell
15   That tolls and tolls, the monotony of fear.

At times we are doctrinaire, at times we are frivolous,
Plastering over the cracks, a gesture making good,
But the strength of us does not come out of us.
It is we, I think, are the idols and it is God
20   Has set us up as men who are painted wood,

And the trains carry us about. But not consistently so,
For during a tiny portion of our lives we are not in trains,
The idol living for a moment, not muscle-bound
But walking freely through the slanting rain,
25   Its ankles wet, its grimace relaxed again.

All over the world people are toasting the King,
Red lozenges of light as each one lifts his glass,
But I will not give you any idol or idea, creed or king,
I give you the incidental things which pass
30   Outward through space exactly as each was.

I give you the disproportion between labour spent
And joy at random; the laughter of the Galway sea
Juggling with spars and bones irresponsibly,
I give you the toy Liffey and the vast gulls,
I give you fuchsia hedges and whitewashed walls.   35

I give you the smell of Norman stone, the squelch
Of bog beneath your boots, the red bog-grass,
The vivid chequer of the Antrim hills, the trough of dark
Golden water for the cart-horses, the brass
Belt of serene sun upon the lough.   40

And I give you the faces, not the permanent masks,
But the faces balanced in the toppling wave—
His glint of joy in cunning as the farmer asks
Twenty per cent too much, or a girl's, forgetting to be
      suave,
A tiro choosing stuffs, preferring mauve.   45

And I give you the sea and yet again the sea's
Tumultuous marble,
With Thor's thunder or taking his ease akimbo,
Lumbering torso, but finger-tips a marvel
Of surgeon's accuracy.   50

I would like to give you more but I cannot hold
This stuff within my hands and the train goes on;
I know that there are further syntheses to which,
Like you perhaps, people at last attain
And find that they are rich and breathing gold.   55

Snow

The room was suddenly rich and the great bay-window
    was
Spawning snow and pink roses against it
Soundlessly collateral and incompatible:
World is suddener than we fancy it.

World is crazier and more of it than we think,
Incorrigibly plural. I peel and portion
A tangerine and spit the pips and feel
The drunkenness of things being various.

And the fire flames with a bubbling sound for world
Is more spiteful and gay than one supposes—
On the tongue on the eyes on the ears in the palms of
    one's hands—
There is more than glass between the snow and the huge
    roses.

Birmingham

Smoke from the train-gulf hid by hoardings blunders
    upward, the brakes of cars
Pipe as the policeman pivoting round raises his flat hand,
    bars
With his figure of a monolith Pharaoh the queue of
    fidgety machines
(Chromium dogs on the bonnet, faces behind the triplex
    screens).
Behind him the streets run away between the proud glass   5
    of shops,
Cubical scent-bottles artificial legs arctic foxes and
    electric mops,
But beyond this centre the slumward vista thins like a
    diagram:
There, unvisited, are Vulcan's forges who doesn't care a
    tinker's damn.

Splayed outwards through the suburbs houses, houses
    for rest
Seducingly rigged by the builder, half-timbered houses   10
    with lips pressed
So tightly and eyes staring at the traffic through bleary
    haws
And only a six-inch grip of the racing earth in their
    concrete claws;
In these houses men as in a dream pursue the Platonic
    Forms
With wireless and cairn terriers and gadgets
    approximating to the fickle norms
And endeavour to find God and score one over the   15
    neighbour

By climbing tentatively upward on jerry-built beauty and
    sweated labour.

The lunch hour: the shops empty, shopgirls' faces relax
Diaphanous as green glass, empty as old almanacs
As incoherent with ticketed geegaws tiered behind their
    heads
20 As the Burne-Jones windows in St Philip's broken by
    crawling leads;
Insipid colour, patches of emotion, Saturday thrills
(This theatre is sprayed with 'June')—the gutter take our
    old playbills,
Next week-end it is likely in the heart's funfair we shall
    pull
Strong enough on the handle to get back our money; or
    at any rate it is possible.

25 On shining lines the trams like vast sarcophagi move
Into the sky, plum after sunset, merging to duck's egg,
    barred with mauve
Zeppelin clouds, and Pentecost-like the cars' headlights
    bud
Out from sideroads and the traffic signals, crême-de-
    menthe or bull's blood,
Tell one to stop, the engine gently breathing, or to go on
30 To where like black pipes of organs in the frayed and
    fading zone
Of the West the factory chimneys on sullen sentry will all
    night wait
To call, in the harsh morning, sleep-stupid faces through
    the daily gate.

Bagpipe Music

It's no go the merrygoround, it's no go the rickshaw,
All we want is a limousine and a ticket for the peepshow.
Their knickers are made of crêpe-de-chine, their shoes
    are made of python,
Their halls are lined with tiger rugs and their walls with
    heads of bison.

John MacDonald found a corpse, put it under the sofa,
Waited till it came to life and hit it with a poker,
Sold its eyes for souvenirs, sold its blood for whiskey,
Kept its bones for dumb-bells to use when he was fifty.

It's no go the Yogi-Man, it's no go Blavatsky,
All we want is a bank balance and a bit of skirt in a taxi.

Annie MacDougall went to milk, caught her foot in the
    heather,
Woke to hear a dance record playing of Old Vienna.
It's no go your maidenheads, it's no go your culture,
All we want is a Dunlop tyre and the devil mend the
    puncture.

The Laird o' Phelps spent Hogmanay declaring he was
    sober,
Counted his feet to prove the fact and found he had one
    foot over.
Mrs Carmichael had her fifth, looked at the job with
    repulsion,
Said to the midwife 'Take it away; I'm through with
    over-production.'

It's no go the gossip-column, it's no go the Ceilidh,
All we want is a mother's help and a sugar-stick for the
baby.

Willie Murray cut his thumb, couldn't count the damage,
Took the hide of an Ayrshire cow and used it for a
bandage.
His brother caught three hundred cran when the seas
were lavish,
Threw the bleeders back in the sea and went upon the
parish.

It's no go the Herring Board, it's no go the Bible,
All we want is a packet of fags when our hands are idle.

It's no go the picture palace, it's no go the stadium,
It's no go the country cot with a pot of pink geraniums,
It's no go the Government grant, it's no go the elections,
Sit on your arse for fifty years and hang your hat on a
pension.

It's no go my honey love, it's no go my poppet;
Work your hands from day to day, the winds will blow
the profit.
The glass is falling hour by hour, the glass will fall for
ever,
But if you break the bloody glass you won't hold up the
weather.

The Sunlight on the Garden

The sunlight on the garden
Hardens and grows cold,
We cannot cage the minute
Within its nets of gold,
When all is told
We cannot beg for pardon.

Our freedom as free lances
Advances towards its end;
The earth compels, upon it
Sonnets and birds descend;
And soon, my friend,
We shall have no time for dances.

The sky was good for flying
Defying the church bells
And every evil iron
Siren and what it tells:
The earth compels,
We are dying, Egypt, dying

And not expecting pardon,
Hardened in heart anew,
But glad to have sat under
Thunder and rain with you,
And grateful too
For sunlight on the garden.

from *Autumn Journal*

V

Today was a beautiful day, the sky was a brilliant
    Blue for the first time for weeks and weeks
But posters flapping on the railings tell the fluttered
    World that Hitler speaks, that Hitler speaks
5 And we cannot take it in and we go to our daily
    Jobs to the dull refrain of the caption 'War'
Buzzing around us as from hidden insects
    And we think 'This must be wrong, it has happened
      before,
Just like this before, we must be dreaming;
10   It was long ago these flies
Buzzed like this, so why are they still bombarding
    The ears if not the eyes?'
And we laugh it off and go round town in the evening
    And this, we say, is on me;
15 Something out of the usual, a Pimm's Number One, a
    Picon—
    But did you see
The latest? You mean whether Cobb has bust the record
    Or do you mean the Australians have lost their last
      by ten
Wickets or do you mean that the autumn fashions—
20   *No, we don't mean anything like that again.*
No, what we mean is Hodza, Henlein, Hitler,
    The Maginot Line,
The heavy panic that cramps the lungs and presses
    The collar down the spine,
25 And when we go out into Piccadilly Circus
    They are selling and buying the late

Special editions snatched and read abruptly
    Beneath the electric signs as crude as Fate.

And the individual, powerless, has to exert the
    Powers of will and choice   30
And choose between enormous evils, either
    Of which depends on somebody else's voice.
The cylinders are racing in the presses,
    The mines are laid,
The ribbon plumbs the fallen fathoms of Wall Street,   35
    And you and I are afraid.
To-day they were building in Oxford Street, the mortar
    Pleasant to smell,
But now it seems futility, imbecility,
    To be building shops when nobody can tell   40
What will happen next. What will happen
    We ask and waste the question on the air;
Nelson is stone and Johnnie Walker moves his
    Legs like a cretin over Trafalgar Square.
And in the Corner House the carpet-sweepers   45
    Advance between the tables after crumbs
Inexorably, like a tank battalion
    In answer to the drums.
In Tottenham Court Road the tarts and negroes
    Loiter beneath the lights   50
And the breeze gets colder as on so many other
    September nights.
A smell of French bread in Charlotte Street, a rustle
    Of leaves in Regent's Park
And suddenly from the Zoo I hear a sea-lion   55
    Confidently bark.
And so to my flat with the trees outside the window
    And the dahlia shapes of the lights on Primrose Hill
Whose summit once was used for a gun emplacement

60   And very likely will
        Be used that way again. The bloody frontier
            Converges on our beds
        Like jungle beaters closing in on their destined
            Trophy of pelts and heads.
65   And at this hour of the day it is no good saying
            'Take away this cup';
        Having helped to fill it ourselves it is only logic
            That now we should drink it up.
        Nor can we hide our heads in the sand, the sands have
70   Filtered away;
        Nothing remains but rock at this hour, this zero
            Hour of the day.
        Or that is how it seems to me as I listen
            To a hooter call at six
        And then a woodpigeon calls and stops but the wind
75   continues
            Playing its dirge in the trees, playing its tricks.
        And now the dairy cart comes clopping slowly—
            Milk at the doors—
        And factory workers are on their way to factories
80   And charwomen to chores.
        And I notice feathers sprouting from the rotted
            Silk of my black
        Double eiderdown which was a wedding
            Present eight years back.
85   And the linen which I lie on came from Ireland
            In the easy days
        When all I thought of was affection and comfort
            Petting and praise.
        And now the woodpigeon starts again denying
90   The values of the town
        And a car having crossed the hill accelerates, changes

Up having just changed down.
And a train begins to chug and I wonder what the
      morning
    Paper will say,
And decide to go quickly to sleep for the morning already   95
    Is with us, the day is to-day.

VII

Conferences, adjournments, ultimatums,
    Flights in the air, castles in the air,
The autopsy of treaties, dynamite under the bridges,
    The end of *laissez-faire*.
After the warm days the rain comes pimpling   5
    The paving stones with white
And with the rain the national conscience, creeping,
    Seeping through the night.
And in the sodden park on Sunday protest
    Meetings assemble not, as so often, now   10
Merely to advertise some patent panacea
    But simply to avow
The need to hold the ditch; a bare avowal
    That may perhaps imply
Death at the doors in a week but perhaps in the long run   15
    Exposure of the lie.
Think of a number, double it, treble it, square it,
    And sponge it out
And repeat *ad lib.* and mark the slate with crosses;
    There is no time to doubt   20
If the puzzle really has an answer. Hitler yells on the
      wireless,
    The night is damp and still
And I hear dull blows on wood outside my window;

They are cutting down the trees on Primrose Hill.
25   The wood is white like the roast flesh of chicken,
        Each tree falling like a closing fan;
No more looking at the view from seats beneath the
        branches,
        Everything is going to plan;
They want the crest of this hill for anti-aircraft,
30   The guns will take the view
And searchlights probe the heavens for bacilli
        With narrow wands of blue.
And the rain came on as I watched the territorials
        Sawing and chopping and pulling on ropes like a
        team
35   In a village tug-of-war; and I found my dog had vanished
        And thought 'This is the end of the old régime,'
But found the police had got her at St John's Wood
        station
        And fetched her in the rain and went for a cup
Of coffee to an all-night shelter and heard a taxi-driver
40   Say 'It turns me up
When I see these soldiers in lorries'—rumble of tumbrils
        Drums in the trees
Breaking the eardrums of the ravished dryads—
        It turns me up; a coffee, please.
45   And as I go out I see a windscreen-wiper
        In an empty car
Wiping away like mad and I feel astounded
        That things have gone so far.
And I come back here to my flat and wonder whether
50   From now on I need take
The trouble to go out choosing stuff for curtains
        As I don't know anyone to make

Curtains quickly. Rather one should quickly
    Stop the cracks for gas or dig a trench
And take one's paltry measures against the coming   55
    Of the unknown Uebermensch.
But one—meaning I—is bored, am bored, the issue
    Involving principle but bound in fact
To squander principle in panic and self-deception—
    Accessories after the act,   60
So that all we foresee is rivers in spate sprouting
    With drowning hands
And men like dead frogs floating till the rivers
    Lose themselves in the sands.
And we who have been brought up to think of 'Gallant   65
        Belgium'
    As so much blague
Are now preparing again to essay good through evil
    For the sake of Prague;
And must, we suppose, become uncritical, vindictive,
    And must, in order to beat   70
The enemy, model ourselves upon the enemy,
    A howling radio for our paraclete.
The night continues wet, the axe keeps falling,
    The hill grows bald and bleak
No longer one of the sights of London but maybe   75
    We shall have fireworks here by this day week.

Prayer Before Birth

I am not yet born; O hear me.
Let not the bloodsucking bat or the rat or the stoat or the
    club-footed ghoul come near me.

I am not yet born, console me.
I fear that the human race may with tall walls wall me,
    with strong drugs dope me, with wise lies lure me,
        on black racks rack me, in blood-baths roll me.

I am not yet born; provide me
With water to dandle me, grass to grow for me, trees to
    talk
        to me, sky to sing to me, birds and a white light
           in the back of my mind to guide me.

I am not yet born; forgive me
For the sins that in me the world shall commit, my words
    when they speak me, my thoughts when they think me,
        my treason engendered by traitors beyond me,
           my life when they murder by means of my
              hands, my death when they live me.

I am not yet born; rehearse me
In the parts I must play and the cues I must take when
    old men lecture me, bureaucrats hector me, mountains
        frown at me, lovers laugh at me, the white
           waves call me to folly and the desert calls
              me to doom and the beggar refuses
                my gift and my children curse me.

I am not yet born; O hear me,
Let not the man who is beast or who thinks he is God
       come near me.

I am not yet born; O fill me
With strength against those who would freeze my
       humanity, would dragoon me into a lethal automaton,
          would make me a cog in a machine, a thing with
             one face, a thing, and against all those
                who would dissipate my entirety, would
                   blow me like thistledown hither and
                      thither or hither and thither
                         like water held in the
                            hands would spill me.

Let them not make me a stone and let them not spill me.
Otherwise kill me.

Glass Falling

The glass is going down. The sun
Is going down. The forecasts say
It will be warm, with frequent showers.
We ramble down the showery hours
And amble up and down the day.
Mary will wear her black goloshes
And splash the puddles on the town;
And soon on fleets of macintoshes
The rain is coming down, the frown
Is coming down of heaven showing
A wet night coming, the glass is going
Down, the sun is going down.

Nuts in May

May come up with bird-din
And May come up with sun-dint,
May come up with water-wheels
    And May come up with iris.

In the sun-peppered meadow the shepherds are old,
Their flutes are broken and their tales are told,
And their ears are deaf when the guns unfold
The new philosophy over the wold.

May come up with pollen of death,
May come up with cordite,
May come up with a chinagraph
 And May come up with a stopwatch.

In the high court of heaven Their tail-feathers shine
With cowspit and bullspit and spirits of wine,
They know no pity, being divine,
And They give no quarter to thine or mine.

May come up with Very lights,
May come up with duty,
May come up with a bouncing cheque,
 An acid-drop and a bandage.

Yes, the angels are frigid and the shepherds are dumb,
There is no holy water when the enemy come,
The trees are askew and the skies are a-hum
And you have to keep mum and go to it and die for your
 life and keep mum.

May come up with fiddle-bows,
May come up with blossom,
May come up the same again,
 The same again but different.

The Back-Again

Back for his holiday from across the water
He fishes with spinners or a rubber eel,
Fishes for mackerel or pollock, but also for something
That he remembers now more by the feel
Of the jigging line than by how it looked when landed.

If it was ever landed. Sitting beside his father,
Whose eyes are smoored with distance, he talks of crops
And weather but would prefer to talk of something
For which he has no words. Till the talk stops
And the fire inside and the rain outside are silent.

And his thoughts return to the city as he fingers
His city tie, thinking he has made good,
Gone up in the world, on the whole, were it not for
    something,
Intuited perhaps though never understood,
Which flitted through this room around his cradle.

So, on his last day, walking beside his brother,
Whose dog like a black thought streaks through ditch and
    fence
Rounding up sheep, he sees in his brother a sudden
    something:
An oaf, but an oaf with dignity and the sense
That it is a fine day if it rains only a little.

The Gone-Tomorrow

Two years high by the world wide,
It scatters pebbles on every side,
It takes two hands to cake or cup,
It pulls the tails of puss and pup.

And the blaze of whins, the smell of turf,
The squelch of mud, the belch of surf,
The slop of porridge, the squawk of gulls,
Enter that smallest of small skulls.

Which some day, skull and nothing more,
Will lie in a box on a foreign shore;
Nor will those empty sockets be,
Like sea-shells, mindful of the sea.

For mottled fields and marbled foam,
Cries of birds and smells of home,
Will all have vanished and the skies
Have lost their blue like those blue eyes.

Notes

WOLVES

Lassitude seems the tone of the first two stanzas: the disillusion of the poet with conventional life-theories is expressed partly in the careless dragging of the verse. In the third stanza the feeling tightens, becomes more urgent: the idea may not appear morally strong, but its strength is in its honesty.

What wolves?

TRAIN TO DUBLIN

A characteristic poem of hedonism imposed upon a profound depression. MacNeice seems unconvinced by talk of human progress or divine significance: but things, happenings and people are worthy of wonder when not forced into theories, but seen simply 'exactly as each was'. (Compare the American Wallace Stevens in Volume One of this series.)

In an unobtrusive way MacNeice is an extraordinarily skilful poet, particularly in apparently effortless and precisely relevant imagery—consider here lines 3, 7, 10, 39-40, 48-49 (what are the finger-tips?).

SNOW

World here, deliberately used with no article, seems to stand for life, the things of this world, all the complexities of existence and perception. Things are not as regular and patterned as we would like them, in our lazier moments, to be: they are 'various'. Notice how ordinary idiom and sentence structure is disturbed in sympathy with the ideas:

> 'World is crazier and more of it than we think,
> Incorrigibly plural.'

The last verse is not easy to paraphrase. The last line but one lists—in an unpunctuated jumble—our senses, our means of perceiving: the last line seems to exhort us to humility and wonder at what we cannot understand.

MacNeice lectured in Classics at Birmingham from 1930 to 1936.

8. *Vulcan* was the tinker or blacksmith god, begrimed and ugly.

10. *rigged*: set up (with a suggestion of *rigged*—cheated. They are not well-built houses, as line 12 shows).

11. *haws*: (i) cartilages in the eye; (ii) hedges.

13. *the Platonic Forms*: noble ideals.

14. *fickle norms*: a norm is a standard or average. Probably MacNeice means the petty fashions to which middle-class people feel the need to conform: a doorbell that chimes, dwarfs in the garden. . . .

15–16. The second half of each line is a studied anti-climax after the first half, just as line 14 deflates line 13. *Sweated labour*—common enough in the 1930's when this poem was written—is work at starvation wages for long hours; workers suffered these terms rather than join the huge numbers of unemployed.

18. *diaphanous*: transparent.

20. *Burne-Jones* was a painter and designer of stained-glass in the late nineteenth century: his work shows indulgent dreamy hazes of sentimental colouring. He was a native of Birmingham, so is doubly appropriate here.

24–5. Throughout the poem the verse is slack and defeated in its movement, like the modern city; but line 24 is a particularly lame example: 'at any rate it is possible' is rhythmically totally apathetic. By contrast, line 25 has a sort of grandeur about it, and indeed MacNeice partially relents, in lines 25–8: the *fauve* colouring of the evening landscape and the grotesque-grandiose comparisons (*sarcophagus*—huge ancient

63

tomb; *Zeppelin*—German cigar-shaped airship; *Pentecost*—referring to the tongues of fire seen on the heads of Christ's disciples) heighten the mood. There is some beauty in the city, and it is of a new, city kind. But the last lines return to the tone of defeat.

BIRMINGHAM is probably MacNeice's wittiest poem—full of subtle twists and neatnesses; but its seriousness is, I think, in no way weakened by that.

BAGPIPE MUSIC
Another musical piece which is also a sketch of the 1930's. *Madame Blavatsky* was a spiritualist and dabbler in the occult who had a large following at the turn of the century. A *Ceilidh* is a Gaelic party.

THE SUNLIGHT ON THE GARDEN
A musical piece rather like some of Auden's (note the intricate rhyme-play) but springier. The tone is characteristic. Of the Oxford poets of the 1930's MacNeice was the least intoxicated by political and humanitarian panaceas, and the most deeply depressed by the signs for the future.
'We are dying, Egypt, dying' is a frivolous theft from ANTONY AND CLEOPATRA: its only possible relevance here is that Antony and Cleopatra enjoyed their hours together before the ultimate defeat and separation.

Extracts from AUTUMN JOURNAL
AUTUMN JOURNAL is a long poem, published as a separate book in 1939: it is a poetic diary of the poet's life in London between August and December 1938. At this time the left-wing cause, which MacNeice and his friends supported, was being defeated in the Spanish Civil War; and elsewhere in Europe Hitler's aggression seemed to make war inevitable. The sections printed here deal with the panic mood of Londoners at the time when Hitler invaded Czechoslovakia and it seemed that Britain must go to war. There is no glory in the

prospect: the First World War was well within memory; and Hitler's Germany was far better equipped and prepared than Britain (this was still true in 1939, when war was eventually declared; but to a lesser extent: the Munich Agreement of autumn 1938 bought Britain a year in which to make ready).

AUTUMN JOURNAL is unique: yet remarkably unpretentious. MacNeice slips into his easy yet disciplined emotional diary as if there were no problems of form or style: he writes straightforwardly and honestly. The poem is not laboriously autobiographical—MacNeice is always shy in this respect—but quietly indicates his own situation and sympathies.

Section V

35. Refers to the tickertape reports of stock-market losses in America.

43-4. *Johnnie Walker . . . cretin*: refers to a neon advertisement for whisky.

Section VII

3. *autopsy*: post-mortem. (The treaties are dead, having been violated.) *dynamite under the bridges*: in readiness to hinder an invading army.

4. *laissez-faire*: here probably means simply a reasonably free society.

41. Soldiers in lorries are perhaps going to their death; tumbrils carried victims to the place of execution.

43. *dryads*: spirits living in trees. During these lines (23–44) MacNeice blends and mixes the felling of the trees, the soldiers, the taxi-driver's remark, and the poet's search for his dog in a general mood-effect of pain and unrest: the terrible image of the windscreen-wiper wiping away unattended brings the distress to a climax.

56. *Uebermensch*: superior people (which Hitler believed the Germans to be).

65-8. 'We who were brought up to look upon the First World War as unnecessary and unheroic, the notion of "Gallant Belgium" (a famous *Punch* cartoon pictured her resisting the Kaiser) as a politician's lie, are now preparing again to try

E   65

to achieve good ends by the use of the evil means of war—for the sake of invaded Czechoslovakia.'

72. *paraclete*: advocate, spokesman.

PRAYER BEFORE BIRTH

MacNeice's most powerful and humane poem: one of that rare kind which seems so necessary and straightforward that one is amazed it had not been written earlier by some other poet. It speaks comprehensively for twentieth-century man.

GLASS FALLING

A musical piece, though with some suggestions of larger issues and deeper depressions than those of mere weather. To study the musical skill of the poem, notice first the various positions in the lines occupied by the repetitions of the word 'down' and the participles 'coming' and 'going'. There is the insistence yet variety of rainfall.

NUTS IN MAY

A 'sick' nursery-rhyme of war. The catchphrases 'keep mum', 'go to it' and 'die for your life' were endlessly reiterated in propaganda during the war.

THE BACK-AGAIN

Remember that MacNeice was an Irishman who spent most of his adult life in London.

The last line gains force if one looks at other poems in which MacNeice uses rain as an uninterpreted symbol—see, in this collection, TRAIN TO DUBLIN (lines 11, 24), BAGPIPE MUSIC (last verse), THE SUNLIGHT ON THE GARDEN, AUTUMN JOURNAL vii (lines 5, 7, 33, 38, 73) and GLASS FALLING.

THE GONE-TOMORROW

whins: gorse.

This short poem brings out more clearly than usual MacNeice's affinity with Thomas Hardy, which it might be worth studying in other poems.

66

Theodore Roethke

Theodore Roethke was born in Michigan in 1908 and educated at the universities of Michigan and Harvard. From 1931 until his death in 1963 he taught English, verse-writing and (at first) tennis, at various colleges and universities in America and Europe. His first book of poetry was published in 1941; but his best work came late in his life, and his reputation is recent and still growing.

Roethke is a poet who goes very much his own way. He shows comparatively little interest in the experiments of his contemporaries, though his work is full of echoes of traditional masters—Blake, Yeats and Whitman in particular. He is a genuine Romantic, more so than most modern poets. Where the early nineteenth-century Romantics reacted sharply against the sophistication of the eighteenth century, Roethke stands in similar contrast to the intellectual ingenuity prevailing in English and American poetry between 1910 and 1940. He is not always an easy poet, but his difficulty lies in the more or less mystical nature of many of his poems (in the same way, Blake's *Songs of Innocence* are particularly difficult poems to discuss).

The soul, spirit, or self is Roethke's principal subject: his material is emotional experience rather than experience logically apprehended. That freshness and wonder which we associate with childhood is present throughout Roethke's work. He revives apparently jaded concepts and forms ('the spirit', or the heavily end-stopped iambic pentameter) without apology or irony, because they are valid for him. The world is seen in its natural essence—the elements, sound, colour, sensation—not politically or sociologically. Other people do not enter into this hermit-like writing, except those with whom the poet is in love. Some poems lack a coherent sequence of thoughts: the reader is required to step, with the poet's nervous groping of mind, from one isolated image to another, and from images recollected from the poet's childhood to those of the present.

Again, Roethke's very use of ancient, essential words and images—above all, those of light and water—presents problems for a modern reader: one has to reach past countless dulled usages to the original brightness of the terms. I am not sure that Roethke can completely succeed, in such consciously archaic work as FOUR FOR SIR JOHN DAVIES, in regaining the freshness which its concepts had for an Elizabethan, or even for Yeats. But at least we should see that what he is trying to do is not a gimmick, nor even an academic indulgence: Roethke as a poet is attempting to say timeless and fundamental things. He is returning to the primary subject-matter of poetry—the relationship of the individual consciousness to the physical facts of its life and its mortality. Sky, water, vegetation, the days and the seasons; childhood, love and death: these are the essential imagery of any such exploration, and Roethke returns to them without embarrassment.

Idyll

Now as from maple to elm the flittermice skitter and
    twirl,
A drunk man stumbles by, absorbed in self-talk.
The lights in the kitchen go out; moth wings unfurl;
The last tricycle runs crazily to the end of the walk.

As darkness creeps up on the well-groomed suburban
    town,
We grow indifferent to dog howls, to the nestling's last
    peep;
Dew deepens on the fresh-cut lawn;
We sit in the porch swing, content and half asleep.

The world recedes in the black revolving shadow;
A far-off train blows its echoing whistle once;
We go to our beds in a house at the edge of a meadow,
Unmindful of terror and headlines, of speeches and guns.

Child on Top of a Greenhouse

The wind billowing out the seat of my britches,
My feet crackling splinters of glass and dried putty,
The half-grown chrysanthemums staring up like accusers,
Up through the streaked glass, flashing with sunlight,
A few white clouds all rushing eastward,
A line of elms plunging and tossing like horses,
And everyone, everyone pointing up and shouting!

Four for Sir John Davies

Is that dance slowing in the mind of man
That made him think the universe could hum?
The great wheel turns its axle when it can;
I need a place to sing, and dancing-room,
5   And I have made a promise to my ears
I'll sing and whistle romping with the bears.

For they are all my friends: I saw one slide
Down a steep hillside on a cake of ice,—
Or was that in a book? I think with pride:
10   A caged bear rarely does the same thing twice
In the same way: O watch his body sway!—
This animal remembering to be gay.

I tried to fling my shadow at the moon,
The while my blood leaped with a wordless song.
15   Though dancing needs a master, I had none
To teach my toes to listen to my tongue.
But what I learned there, dancing all alone,
Was not the joyless motion of a stone.

I take this cadence from a man named Yeats;
20   I take it, and I give it back again:
For other times and other wanton beats
Have tossed my heart and fiddled through my brain.
Yes, I was dancing-mad, and how
That came to be the bears and Yeats would know.

II. *The Partner*

Between such animal and human heat   25
I find myself perplexed. What is desire?
The impulse to make someone else complete?
That woman would set sodden straw on fire.
Was I the servant of a sovereign wish,
Or ladle rattling in an empty dish?   30

We played a measure with commingled feet:
The lively dead had taught us to be fond.
Who can embrace the body of his fate?
Light altered light along the living ground.
She kissed me close, and then did something else.   35
My marrow beat as wildly as my pulse.

I'd say it to my horse: we live beyond
Our outer skin. Who's whistling up my sleeve?
I see a heron prancing in his pond;
I know a dance the elephants believe.   40
The living all assemble! What's the cue?—
Do what the clumsy partner wants to do!

Things loll and loiter. Who condones the lost?
This joy outleaps the dog. Who cares? Who cares?
I gave her kisses back, and woke a ghost.   45
O what lewd music crept into our ears!
The body and the soul know how to play
In that dark world where gods have lost their way.

III. *The Wraith*

Incomprehensible gaiety and dread
50　Attended what we did. Behind, before,
Lay all the lonely pastures of the dead;
The spirit and the flesh cried out for more.
We two, together, on a darkening day
Took arms against our own obscurity.

55　Did each become the other in that play?
She laughed me out, and then she laughed me in;
In the deep middle of ourselves we lay;
When glory failed, we danced upon a pin.
The valley rocked beneath the granite hill;
60　Our souls looked forth, and the great day stood still.

There was a body, and it cast a spell,—
God pity those but wanton to the knees,—
The flesh can make the spirit visible;
We woke to find the moonlight on our toes.
65　In the rich weather of a dappled wood
We played with dark and light as children should.

What shape leaped forward at the sensual cry?—
Sea-beast or bird flung towards the ravaged shore?
Did space shake off an angel with a sigh?
70　We rose to meet the moon, and saw no more.
It was and was not she, a shape alone,
Impaled on light, and whirling slowly down.

IV. *The Vigil*

Dante attained the purgatorial hill,
Trembled at hidden virtue without flaw,
Shook with a mighty power beyond his will,—   75
Did Beatrice deny what Dante saw?
All lovers live by longing, and endure:
Summon a vision and declare it pure.

Though everything's astonishment at last,
Who leaps to heaven at a single bound?   80
The links were soft between us; still, we kissed;
We undid chaos to a curious sound:
The waves broke easy, cried to me in white;
Her look was morning in the dying light.

The visible obscures. But who knows when?   85
Things have their thought: they are the shards of me;
I thought that once, and thought comes round again;
Rapt, we leaned forth with what we could not see.
We danced to shining; mocked before the black
And shapeless night that made no answer back.   90

The world is for the living. Who are they?
We dared the dark to reach the white and warm.
She was the wind when wind was in my way;
Alive at noon, I perished in her form.
Who rise from flesh to spirit know the fall: 95
The word outleaps the world, and light is all.

A Field of Light

I

Came to lakes; came to dead water,
Ponds with moss and leaves floating,
Planks sunk in the sand.

A log turned at the touch of a foot;
A long weed floated upward;
An eye tilted.

Small winds made
A chilly noise;
The softest cove
Cried for sound.

Reached for a grape
And the leaves changed;
A stone's shape
Became a clam.

A fine rain fell
On fat leaves;
I was there alone
In a watery drowse.

II

Angel within me, I asked,
Did I ever curse the sun?
Speak and abide.

Under, under the sheaves,
Under the blackened leaves,
Behind the green viscid trellis,
In the deep grass at the edge of field,
Along the low ground dry only in August,—

Was it dust I was kissing?
A sigh came far.
Alone, I kissed the skin of a stone;
Marrow-soft, danced in the sand.

III

The dirt left my hand, visitor.
I could feel the mare's nose.
A path went walking.

The sun glittered on a small rapids.
Some morning thing came, beating its wings.
The great elm filled with birds.

Listen, love,
The fat lark sang in the field;
I touched the ground, the ground warmed by the
        killdeer,
The salt laughed and the stones;
The ferns had their ways, and the pulsing lizards,
And the new plants, still awkward in their soil,
The lovely diminutives.
I could watch! I could watch!
I saw the separateness of all things!
My heart lifted up with the great grasses;

The weeds believed me, and the nesting birds.
There were clouds making a rout of shapes crossing
a windbreak of cedars,
And a bee shaking drops from a rain-soaked honey-
suckle.
The worms were delighted as wrens.
And I walked, I walked through the light air;
I moved with the morning.

Meditation at Oyster River

I

Over the low, barnacled, elephant-coloured rocks,
Come the first tide-ripples, moving, almost without
    sound, towards me,
Running along the narrow furrows of the shore, the rows
    of dead clam shells;
Then a runnel behind me, creeping closer,
Alive with tiny striped fish, and young crabs climbing in
    and out of the water.

No sound from the bay. No violence.
Even the gulls quiet on the far rocks,
Silent, in the deepening light,
Their cat-mewing over,
Their child-whimpering.

At last one long undulant ripple,
Blue-black from where I am sitting,
Makes almost a wave over a barrier of small stones,
Slapping lightly against a sunken log.
I dabble my toes in the brackish foam sliding forward,
Then retire to a rock higher up on the cliff-side.
The wind slackens, light as a moth fanning a stone:
A twilight wind, light as a child's breath
Turning not a leaf, not a ripple.
The dew revives on the beach-grass;
The salt-soaked wood of a fire crackles;
A fish raven turns on its perch (a dead tree in the river-
    mouth),
Its wings catching a last glint of the reflected sunlight.

77

The self persists like a dying star,
In sleep, afraid. Death's face rises afresh,
Among the shy beasts, the deer at the salt-lick,
The doe with its sloped shoulders loping across the high-
　　way,
The young snake, poised in green leaves, waiting for its
　　fly,
The hummingbird, whirring from quince-blossom to
　　morning-glory—
With these I would be.
And with water: the waves coming forward, without
　　cessation,
The waves, altered by sand-bars, beds of kelp, miscel-
　　laneous driftwood,
Topped by crosswinds, tugged at by sinuous under-
　　currents
The tide rustling in, sliding between the ridges of stone,
The tongues of water, creeping in, quietly.

III

In this hour,
In this first heaven of knowing,
The flesh takes on the pure poise of the spirit,
Acquires, for a time, the sandpiper's insouciance,
The hummingbird's surety, the kingfisher's cunning—
I shift on my rock, and I think:
Of the first trembling of a Michigan brook in April,
Over a lip of stone, the tiny rivulet;
And that wrist-thick cascade tumbling from a cleft rock,
Its spray holding a double rain-bow in early morning,

Small enough to be taken in, embraced, by two arms,—
Or the Tittebawasee, in the time between winter and
    spring,
When the ice melts along the edges in early afternoon.
And the midchannel begins cracking and heaving from
    the pressure beneath,
The ice piling high against the iron-bound spiles,
Gleaming, freezing hard again, creaking at midnight—
And I long for the blast of dynamite,
The sudden sucking roar as the culvert loosens its debris
    of branches and sticks,
Welter of tin cans, pails, old bird nests, a child's shoe
    riding a log,
As the piled ice breaks away from the battered spiles,
And the whole river begins to move forward, its bridges
    shaking.

IV

Now, in this waning of light,
I rock with the motion of morning;
In the cradle of all that is,
I'm lulled into half-sleep
By the lapping of water,
Cries of the sandpiper.
Water's my will, and my way,
And the spirit runs, intermittently,
In and out of the small waves,
Runs with the intrepid shorebirds—
How graceful the small before danger!

In the first of the moon,
All's a scattering,
A shining.

The Far Field

I

I dream of journeys repeatedly:
Of flying like a bat deep into a narrowing tunnel,
Of driving alone, without luggage, out a long peninsula,
The road lined with snow-laden second growth,
A fine dry snow ticking the windshield,
Alternate snow and sleet, no on-coming traffic,
And no lights behind, in the blurred side-mirror,
The road changing from glazed tarface to a rubble of
    stone,
Ending at last in a hopeless sand-rut,
Where the car stalls,
Churning in a snowdrift
Until the headlights darken.

II

At the field's end, in the corner missed by the mower,
Where the turf drops off into a grass-hidden culvert,
Haunt of the cat-bird, nesting-place of the field-mouse,
Not too far away from the ever-changing flower-dump,
Among the tin cans, tires, rusted pipes, broken
    machinery,—
One learned of the eternal;
And in the shrunken face of a dead rat, eaten by rain and
    ground-beetles
(I found it lying among the rubble of an old coal bin)
And the tom-cat, caught near the pheasant-run,
Its entrails strewn over the half-grown flowers,
Blasted to death by the night-watchman.

I suffered for birds, for young rabbits caught in the
    mower,
My grief was not excessive.
For to come upon warblers in early May
Was to forget time and death:
How they filled the oriole's elm, a twittering restless
    cloud, all one morning,
And I watched and watched till my eyes blurred from the
    bird shapes,—
Cape May, Blackburnian, Cerulean,—
Moving, elusive as fish, fearless,
Hanging, bunched like young fruit, bending the end
    branches,
Still for a moment,
Then pitching away in half-flight,
Lighter than finches,
While the wrens bickered and sang in the half-green
    hedgerows,
And the flicker drummed from his dead tree in the
    chicken-yard.

—Or to lie naked in sand,
In the silted shallows of a slow river,
Fingering a shell,
Thinking:
Once I was something like this, mindless,
Or perhaps with another mind, less peculiar;
Or to sink down to the hips in a mossy quagmire;
Or, with skinny knees, to sit astride a wet log,
Believing:
I'll return again,
As a snake or a raucous bird,
Or, with luck, as a lion.

F   81

I learned not to fear infinity,
The far field, the windy cliffs of forever,
The dying of time in the white light of tomorrow,
The wheel turning away from itself,
The sprawl of the wave,
The on-coming water.

III

The river turns on itself,
The tree retreats into its own shadow.
I feel a weightless change, a moving forward
As of water quickening before a narrowing channel
When banks converge, and the wide river whitens;
Or when two rivers combine, the blue glacial torrent
And the yellowish-green from the mountainy upland,—
At first a swift rippling between rocks,
Then a long running over flat stones
Before descending to the alluvial plain,
To the clay banks, and the wild grapes hanging from the
    elmtrees,
The slightly trembling water
Dropping a fine yellow silt where the sun stays;
And the crabs bask near the edge,
The weedy edge, alive with small snakes and blood
    suckers,—
I have come to a still, but not a deep centre,
A point outside the glittering current;
My eyes stare at the bottom of a river,
At the irregular stones, iridescent sandgrains,
My mind moves in more than one place,
In a country half-land, half-water.

I am renewed by death, thought of my death,
The dry scent of a dying garden in September,
The wind fanning the ash of a low fire.
What I love is near at hand,
Always, in earth and air.

IV

The lost self changes,
Turning towards the sea,
A sea-shape turning around,—
An old man with his feet before the fire,
In robes of green, in garments of adieu.

A man faced with his own immensity
Wakes all the waves, all their loose wandering fire.
The murmur of the absolute, the why
Of being born fails on his naked ears.
His spirit moves like monumental wind
That gentles on a sunny blue plateau.
He is the end of things, the final man.

All finite things reveal infinitude:
The mountain with its singular bright shade
Like the blue shine on freshly frozen snow,
The after-light upon ice-burdened pines;
Odour of basswood on a mountain-slope,
A scent beloved of bees;
Silence of water above a sunken tree:
The pure serene of memory in one man,—
A ripple widening from a single stone
Winding around the waters of the world.

The Thing

Suddenly they came flying, like a long scarf of smoke,
Trailing a thing—what was it?—small as a lark
Above the blue air, in the slight haze beyond,
A thing in and out of sight,
Flashing between gold levels of the late sun,
Then throwing itself up and away from the implacable
    swift pursuers,
Confusing them once flying straight into the sun
So they circled aimlessly for almost a minute,
Only to find, with their long terrible eyes
The small thing diving down towards a hill,
Where they dropped again
In one streak of pursuit.

Then the first bird
Struck;
Then another, another,
Until there was nothing left,
Not even feathers from so far away.

And we turned to our picnic
Of veal soaked in marsala and little larks arranged on a
    long platter;
And we drank the dry harsh wine
While I poked with a stick at a stone near a four-pronged
    flower,
And a black bull nudged at a wall in the valley below,
And the blue air darkened.

The Sequel

I

Was I too glib about eternal things,
An intimate of air and all its songs?
Pure aimlessness pursued and yet pursued
And all wild longings of the insatiate blood
Brought me down to my knees. O who can be
Both moth and flame? The weak moth blundering by.
Whom do we love? I thought I knew the truth;
Of grief I died, but no one knew my death.

II

I saw a body dancing in the wind,
A shape called up out of my natural mind;
I heard a bird stir in its true confine;
A nestling sighed—I called that nestling mine;
A partridge drummed; a minnow nudged its stone;
We danced, we danced, under a dancing moon;
And on the coming of the outrageous dawn,
We danced together, we danced on and on.

III

Morning's a motion in a happy mind:
She stayed in light, as leaves live in the wind,
Swaying in air, like some long water weed.
She left my body, lighter than a seed;
I gave her body full and grave farewell.
A wind came close, like a shy animal.
A light leaf on a tree, she swayed away
To the dark beginnings of another day.

IV

Was nature kind? The heart's core tractable?
All waters waver, and all fires fail.
Leaves, leaves lean forth and tell me what I am;
This single tree turns into purest flame.
I am a man, a man at intervals
Pacing a room, a room with dead-white walls;
I feel the autumn fail—all that slow fire
Denied in me, who has denied desire.

The Tree, The Bird

Uprose, uprose, the stony fields uprose,
And every snail dipped towards me its pure horn.
The sweet light met me as I walked towards
A small voice calling from a drifting cloud.
I was a finger pointing at the moon,
At ease with joy, a self-enchanted man.
Yet when I sighed, I stood outside my life,
A leaf unaltered by the midnight scene,
Part of a tree still dark, still, deathly still,
Riding the air, a willow with its kind,
Bearing its life and more, a double sound,
Kin to the wind, and the bleak whistling rain.

The willow with its bird grew loud, grew louder still.
I could not bear its song, that altering
With every shift of air, those beating wings,
The lonely buzz behind my midnight eyes;—
How deep the mother-root of that still cry!

The present falls, the present falls away;
How pure the motion of the rising day,
The white sea widening on a farther shore.
The bird, the beating bird, extending wings—.
Thus I endure this last pure stretch of joy,
The dire dimension of a final thing.

Notes

IDYLL

From Roethke's first book, where the poems are terse, neatly stanzaic, using rhyme and half-rhyme, IDYLL should be taken, I think, exactly as it stands: a clear picture of ordinary twentieth-century life, 'well-groomed' and leisured, but never completely free of the uneasy, sinister things mentioned in the last verse (for it seems that to be 'unmindful of terror and headlines, of speeches and guns' is itself to be in an 'idyll').

flittermice are bats.

CHILD ON TOP OF A GREENHOUSE

A moment recollected: the fragmentary nature of excitement (and of recollection) is caught in the verbs, which are all in a participial form—incomplete.

FOUR FOR SIR JOHN DAVIES

Sir John Davies was an Elizabethan poet, one of whose poems, *Orchestra* (written in seven-line stanzas to which Roethke's six-line stanzas bear considerable resemblance), expresses a medieval theory that the universe operates in one great ordered movement or dance. There *is* an ultimate control and pattern, there is spiritual reality as well as physical reality—all aspects of experience have their place.

Roethke 'offers' to Sir John Davies four twentieth-century poems which attempt to rediscover that total acceptance of love, both physical and spiritual, which distinguishes the best Elizabethan writing. The first poem, THE DANCE, does not mention the loved one; but she is there by implication. In the modern world of declining belief in eternal values or eternal order, the poet feels himself unnecessarily fettered: his emotions are on too grand a scale, he says, for this. He wants to attain ecstasy, the soul dancing with the universe: an idea which is today so unfashionable. There is a reference to Yeats, who in SAILING TO BYZANTIUM sought for teachers who would instruct his soul to 'clap its hands and sing'. The bears are perhaps slightly cosy and literary ('Or was that in a book?').

The remaining three poems show how physical passion can lead to the highest mysteries. Yet desire is puzzling, and the poems recapture the agitation of physical excitement rather than a tranquil or coherent philosophy.

Line 28 is a refutation of the theory advanced in line 27.

31. *measure*: a dance-step.

49–51. Love is the most *living* of all acts: to experience it is to be most vividly aware of inevitable death. (Compare lines 32, 33, 41, 45.)

54. *obscurity*: darkness (i.e. death).

64. Why *toes*?

65–6. For 'dark and light' (making the 'dappled wood' of experience) see lines 34 and 45, and, below, 89–90, 92.

67–72. An attempt to state the mystical exaltation of lovers.

76. *Beatrice*: the poet Dante's beloved.

82. *undid chaos*: perhaps, made form and coherence.

84. *morning . . . dying light*: compare the contradictions of 32 and 66.

85. *obscures*: compare line 54.

86. *shards*: fragments.

95. A difficult line. 'Fall' balances 'rise' in contradiction: there may be some suggestion of 'The Fall' (Adam and Eve in the Garden), but more probably the line means 'the lovers who pass by fleshly love into spiritual love understand the nature of death'. Line 96 suggests that they indeed attain heaven (see the use of 'leapt' in line 80).

A FIELD OF LIGHT
A poem composed entirely of images from physical experience, probably in childhood. Roethke is feeling for a cryptic

clarity like that of Blake; and asserting *things* rather than *thoughts*. Such a poem demands a certain acceptance on the reader's part: it is an act of courage in a modern poet to write in so vulnerable a manner.

> Small winds made
> A chilly noise . . .

> . . . The weeds believed me . . .

Some readers, confronted by poetry like this (or 'naive' painting) suspect fraud, and are determinedly sceptical. Test the honesty of this poem by testing the details of its expression: 'the skin of a stone' . . . 'the fat leaves' . . . 'A path went walking'. . . .

What the poem *means* is hard to say; what it *is* seems vivid and clear enough.

MEDITATION AT OYSTER RIVER

This and the rest of the poems in this selection are late poems, first published after Roethke's death. MEDITATION AT OYSTER RIVER and THE FAR FIELD are from a group of poems called NORTH AMERICAN SEQUENCE, which look more or less consciously to Whitman for their guide. But if you have not read Whitman's poetry, it hardly matters (whereas it certainly is a help, elsewhere in Roethke, to know something of Blake and Yeats). The lines are long and leisurely, but have all the incantatory quality that goes with verse.

Here, in the most basic Romantic sense, the poet wants to be 'at one with nature'. He appears disturbed by his human consciousness of himself and of his inevitable death; by contrast animals, or water, have no such sense of themselves, and no such knowledge. They live consistently and surely the physical life of the world.

In section III the poet involves himself entirely with the image of water, as it comes to life after winter; and in section IV he seems, as a result of that contemplation, eased and reconciled. The pianissimo ending has a delicacy one rarely finds in Whitman.

kelp is seaweed; *spiles* are timbers driven into the ground, presumably at the water's edge; a *culvert* is a drainage channel.

THE FAR FIELD

One of Roethke's most straightforward poems, and one of his most memorable. The poet faces his own death, calmly. Section one offers a claustrophobic metaphor for death; section two a reminiscence (as so often in Roethke) of childhood, where his instinctive trust in the processes of living and dying was developed. In the third section he states, as clearly as is reasonably possible, his preparedness for death. Finally he expresses the sense of completion—and of the infinite—which he gains from being prepared for death.

Throughout the imagery is that closely observed imagery of the real world which has steadily become more and more important in Roethke's poetry as he grows older; but he can also offer us great abstract lines in a classic manner:

The far field, the windy cliffs of forever,
The dying of time in the white light of tomorrow.

One such line, 'All finite things reveal infinitude', might stand as a motto for all Roethke's poetry.

THE THING

An incident observed, in Italy. The cruelty of natural things is ironically capped by the picnic ('and little larks arranged on a long platter'). The black bull seems almost a symbol of that cruelty. The air, for the poet at least, darkens. . . .

THE SEQUEL

The same imagery of dance, morning and light as in FOUR FOR SIR JOHN DAVIES is used. The meaning of this poem is elusive, but it is clearly a less confident and cheerful statement than that earlier work: a loved one has left the poet, but the last lines of the poem suggest that the fault is his. In some way he has 'denied desire'. The loved one is perhaps not a person, but a basic confidence or faith in which he could earlier exult. Certainly he speaks, in this poem, as a man dashed and humbled.

THE TREE, THE BIRD

A poem (I think) about dying. The willow tree, traditionally melancholy or sinister, and the birdsong within it, are 'still dark, still, deathly still', and are outside the poet's life of joy and 'sweet light'. In the central section they overwhelm him, and here perhaps Roethke anticipates his death. In the last section the poet, still alive, cherishes the last moments of life more keenly than ever for the knowledge of the beating wings behind his eyes.

This is an explanation; though I cannot be certain it is right. Nor am I sure whether 'that still cry' (line 17) refers to the bird or (more probably) to the angel-voice 'calling from a drifting cloud' (line 4).

Dylan Thomas

Dylan Thomas was born in 1914 in South Wales, and was educated at a grammar school in Swansea. His first book of poetry was published when he was only nineteen, and he became rapidly known and lionized. He lived by writing, for the B.B.C., newspapers and films, and—in later years—by poetry readings, especially in the United States; but this public life took a severe toll of both his health and his poetry. He died in America in 1953.

Thomas has sometimes been linked by critics with the Surrealist painters: his writing uses conventional structures, but by irrational associations of words is confusing, and it makes much use of instinctive psychological symbolism, much of it more or less sexual. But Thomas was an explosive, ebullient character, and the logic of his symbolism is hardly more coherent than that of his explicit statements. His strengths are in the bravado of his diction and imagery and the incantatory power of his verse, which is a sort of broad popularized pastiche of Shakespeare, Gerard Manley Hopkins and W. B. Yeats.

Thomas is still not an easy poet to assess calmly, for his reputation was dangerously inflated during the 1950's and there is an equally strong reaction against him now. The case against him is that the ideas behind his poetry are hard to grasp, and, when grasped, unimpressive; that his imagery is grossly oversized and clumsily handled, and the 'music' of his verse the crudest of chimings and conventional pentameters. The case in his favour is that he is a poetic personality undeniably distinct from his contemporaries, that his best work captures psychological moods which have been rarely captured, especially those of childhood and adolescence, and that

93

he represents a bold and welcome attempt to achieve a twentieth-century rhetoric, refusing to believe that all modern poetry should be drab, conversational and rational.

'The force that through the green fuse drives the flower...'

The force that through the green fuse drives the flower
Drives my green age; that blasts the roots of trees
Is my destroyer.
And I am dumb to tell the crooked rose
My youth is bent by the same wintry fever.

The force that drives the water through the rocks
Drives my red blood; that dries the mouthing streams
Turns mine to wax.
And I am dumb to mouth unto my veins
How at the mountain spring the same mouth sucks.

The hand that whirls the water in the pool
Stirs the quicksand; that ropes the blowing wind
Hauls my shroud sail.
And I am dumb to tell the hanging man
How of my clay is made the hangman's lime.

The lips of time leech to the fountain-head;
Love drips and gathers, but the fallen blood
Shall calm her sores.
And I am dumb to tell a weather's wind
How time has ticked a heaven round the stars.

And I am dumb to tell the lover's tomb
How at my sheet goes the same crooked worm.

'Light breaks where no sun shines . . .'

Light breaks where no sun shines;
Where no sea runs, the waters of the heart
Push in their tides;
And, broken ghosts with glowworms in their heads,
The things of light
File through the flesh where no flesh decks the bones.

A candle in the thighs
Warms youth and seed and burns the seeds of age;
Where no seed stirs,
The fruit of man unwrinkles in the stars,
Bright as a fig;
Where no wax is, the candle shows its hairs.

Dawn breaks behind the eyes;
From poles of skull and toe the windy blood
Slides like a sea;
Nor fenced, nor staked, the gushers of the sky
Spout to the rod
Divining in a smile the oil of tears.

Night in the sockets rounds,
Like some pitch moon, the limit of the globes;
Day lights the bone;
Where no cold is, the skinning gales unpin
The winter's robes;
The film of spring is hanging from the lids.

Light breaks on secret lots,
On tips of thought where thoughts smell in the rain;
When logics die,
The secret of the soil grows through the eye,
And blood jumps in the sun;
Above the waste allotments the dawn halts.

In Memory of Ann Jones

After the funeral, mule praises, brays,
Windshake of sailshaped ears, muffle-toed tap
Tap happily of one peg in the thick
Grave's foot, blinds down the lids, the teeth in black,
The spittled eyes, the salt ponds in the sleeves,
Morning smack of the spade that wakes up sleep,
Shakes a desolate boy who slits his throat
In the dark of the coffin and sheds dry leaves
That breaks one bone to light with a judgment clout,
After the feast of tear-stuffed time and thistles
In a room with a stuffed fox and a stale fern,
I stand, for this memorial's sake, alone
In the snivelling hours with dead, humped Ann
Whose hooded, fountain heart once fell in puddles
Round the parched world of Wales and drowned each sun
(Though this for her is a monstrous image blindly
Magnified out of praise; her death was a still drop;
She would not have me sinking in the holy
Flood of her heart's fame; she would lie dumb and deep
And need no druid of her broken body).
But I, Ann's bard on a raised hearth, call all
The seas to service that her wood-tongued virtue
Babble like a bellbuoy over the hymning heads,

Bow down the walls of the ferned and foxy woods
That her love sing and swing through a brown chapel,
Bless her bent spirit with four, crossing birds.
Her flesh was meek as milk, but this skyward statue
With the wild breast and blessed and giant skull
Is carved from her in a room with a wet window
In a fiercely mourning house in a crooked year.
I know her scrubbed and sour humble hands
Lie with religion in their cramp, her threadbare
Whisper in a damp word, her wits drilled hollow,
Her fist of a face died clenched on a round pain;
And sculptured Ann is seventy years of stone.
These cloud-sopped, marble hands, this monumental
Argument of the hewn voice, gesture and psalm
Storm me forever over her grave until
The stuffed lung of the fox twitch and cry Love
And the strutting fern lay seeds on the black sill.

The Conversation of Prayer

The conversation of prayers about to be said
By the child going to bed and the man on the stairs
Who climbs to his dying love in her high room,
The one not caring to whom in his sleep he will move
And the other full of tears that she will be dead,

Turns in the dark on the sound they know will arise
Into the answering skies from the green ground,
From the man on the stairs and the child by his bed.
The sound about to be said in the two prayers
For the sleep in a safe land and the love who dies

Will be the same grief flying. Whom shall they calm?
Shall the child sleep unharmed or the man be crying?
The conversation of prayers about to be said
Turns on the quick and the dead, and the man on the
    stairs
To night shall find no dying but alive and warm

In the fire of his care his love in the high room.
And the child not caring to whom he climbs his prayer
Shall drown in a grief as deep as his true grave,
And mark the dark eyed wave, through the eyes of sleep,
Dragging him up the stairs to one who lies dead.

A Refusal to Mourn the Death, by Fire, of a Child in London

Never until the mankind making
Bird beast and flower
Fathering and all humbling darkness
Tells with silence the last light breaking
And the still hour
Is come of the sea tumbling in harness

And I must enter again the round
Zion of the water bead
And the synagogue of the ear of corn
Shall I let pray the shadow of a sound
Or sow my salt seed
In the least valley of sackcloth to mourn

The majesty and burning of the child's death.
I shall not murder
The mankind of her going with a grave truth
Nor blaspheme down the stations of the breath
With any further
Elegy of innocence and youth.

Deep with the first dead lies London's daughter,
Robed in the long friends,
The grains beyond age, the dark veins of her mother,
Secret by the unmourning water
Of the riding Thames.
After the first death, there is no other.

Poem in October

It was my thirtieth year to heaven
Woke to my hearing from harbour and neighbour wood
    And the mussel pooled and the heron
        Priested shore
        The morning beckon
With water praying and call of seagull and rook
And the knock of sailing boats on the net webbed wall
        Myself to set foot
        That second
In the still sleeping town and set forth.

My birthday began with the water-
Birds and the birds of the winged trees flying my name
    Above the farms and the white horses
        And I rose
        In rainy autumn
And walked abroad in a shower of all my days.
High tide and the heron dived when I took the road
        Over the border
        And the gates
Of the town closed as the town awoke.

A springful of larks in a rolling
Cloud and the roadside bushes brimming with whistling
    Blackbirds and the sun of October
        Summery
        On the hill's shoulder,
Here were fond climates and sweet singers suddenly
Come in the morning where I wandered and listened
        To the rain wringing
        Wind blow cold
In the wood faraway under me.

Pale rain over the dwindling harbour
And over the sea wet church the size of a snail
With its horns through mist and the castle
Brown as owls
But all the gardens
Of spring and summer were blooming in the tall tales
Beyond the border and under the lark full cloud
There could I marvel
My birthday
Away but the weather turned around.

It turned away from the blithe country
And down the other air and the blue altered sky
Streamed again a wonder of summer
With apples
Pears and red currants
And I saw in the turning so clearly a child's
Forgotten mornings when he walked with his mother
Through the parables
Of sun light
And the legends of the green chapels

And the twice told fields of infancy
That his tears burned my cheeks and his heart moved in
mine.
These were the woods the river and sea
Where a boy
In the listening
Summertime of the dead whispered the truth of his joy
To the trees and the stones and the fish in the tide.
And the mystery
Sang alive
Still in the water and singingbirds.

And there could I marvel my birthday
Away but the weather turned around. And the true
   Joy of the long dead child sang burning
      In the sun.
     It was my thirtieth
Year to heaven stood there then in the summer noon
Though the town below lay leaved with October blood.
     O may my heart's truth
      Still be sung
On this high hill in a year's turning.

This side of the Truth

(For Llewelyn)

This side of the truth,
You may not see, my son,
King of your blue eyes
In the blinding country of youth,
That all is undone,
Under the unminding skies,
Of innocence and guilt
Before you move to make
One gesture of the heart or head,
Is gathered and spilt
Into the winding dark
Like the dust of the dead.

Good and bad, two ways
Of moving about your death
By the grinding sea,
King of your heart in the blind days,

103

Blow away like breath,
Go crying through you and me

And the souls of all men
Into the innocent
Dark, and the guilty dark, and good
Death, and bad death, and then
In the last element
Fly like the stars' blood,

Like the sun's tears,
Like the moon's seed, rubbish
And fire, the flying rant
Of the sky, king of your six years.
And the wicked wish,
Down the beginning of plants
And animals and birds,
Water and light, the earth and sky,
Is cast before you move,
And all your deeds and words,
Each truth, each lie,
Die in unjudging love.

On a Wedding Anniversary

The sky is torn across
This ragged anniversary of two
Who moved for three years in tune
Down the long walks of their vows.

Now their love lies a loss
And Love and his patients roar on a chain;
From every true or crater
Carrying cloud, Death strikes their house.

Too late in the wrong rain
They come together whom their love parted:
The windows pour into their heart
And the doors burn in their brain.

The Hunchback in the Park

The hunchback in the park
A solitary mister
Propped between trees and water
From the opening of the garden lock
That lets the trees and water enter
Until the Sunday sombre bell at dark

Eating bread from a newspaper
Drinking water from the chained cup
That the children filled with gravel
In the fountain basin where I sailed my ship
Slept at night in a dog kennel
But nobody chained him up.

Like the park birds he came early
Like the water he sat down
And Mister they called Hey mister
The truant boys from the town
Running when he had heard them clearly
On out of sound

Past lake and rockery
Laughing when he shook his paper
Hunchbacked in mockery
Through the loud zoo of the willow groves
Dodging the park keeper
With his stick that picked up leaves.

And the old dog sleeper
Alone between nurses and swans
While the boys among the willows
Made the tigers jump out of their eyes
To roar on the rockery stones
And the groves were blue with sailors

Made all day until bell time
A woman figure without fault
Straight as a young elm
Straight and tall from his crooked bones
That she might stand in the night
After the locks and chains

All night in the unmade park
After the railings and shrubberies
The birds the grass the trees the lake
And the wild boys innocent as strawberries
Had followed the hunchback
To his kennel in the dark.

In my Craft or Sullen Art

In my craft or sullen art
Exercised in the still night
When only the moon rages
And the lovers lie abed
With all their griefs in their arms,
I labour by singing light
Not for ambition or bread
Or the strut and trade of charms
On the ivory stages
But for the common wages
Of their most secret heart.

Not for the proud man apart
From the raging moon I write
On these spindrift pages
Nor for the towering dead
With their nightingales and psalms
But for the lovers, their arms
Round the griefs of the ages,
Who pay no praise or wages
Nor heed my craft or art.

Among those killed in the dawn raid
was a man aged a hundred

When the morning was waking over the war
He put on his clothes and stepped out and he died,
The locks yawned loose and a blast blew them wide,
He dropped where he loved on the burst pavement stone
And the funeral grains of the slaughtered floor.
Tell his street on its back he stopped a sun
And the craters of his eyes grew springshoots and fire
When all the keys shot from the locks, and rang.
Dig no more for the chains of his grey-haired heart.
The heavenly ambulance drawn by a wound
Assembling waits for the spade's ring on the cage.
O keep his bones away from that common cart,
The morning is flying on the wings of his age
And a hundred storks perch on the sun's right hand.

Fern Hill

Now as I was young and easy under the apple boughs
About the lilting house and happy as the grass was green,
    The night above the dingle starry,
        Time let me hail and climb
    Golden in the heydays of his eyes,
And honoured among wagons I was prince of the apple
            towns
And once below a time I lordly had the trees and leaves
        Trail with daisies and barley
    Down the rivers of the windfall light

And as I was green and carefree, famous among the
        barns
About the happy yard and singing as the farm was home,
    In the sun that is young once only,
        Time let me play and be
        Golden in the mercy of his means,
And green and golden I was huntsman and herdsman,
        the calves
Sang to my horn, the foxes on the hills barked clear and
        cold,
        And the sabbath rang slowly
    In the pebbles of the holy streams.

All the sun long it was running, it was lovely, the hay
Fields high as the house, the tunes from the chimneys, it
        was air
        And playing, lovely and watery
        And fire green as grass.
    And nightly under the simple stars
As I rode to sleep the owls were bearing the farm away,
All the moon long I heard, blessed among stables, the
        nightjars
        Flying with the ricks, and the horses
        Flashing into the dark.

And then to awake, and the farm, like a wanderer white
With the dew, come back, the cock on his shoulder; it
        was all
        Shining, it was Adam and maiden,
        The sky gathered again
    And the sun grew round that very day.
So it must have been after the birth of the simple light

In the first, spinning place, the spellbound horses walking
          warm
     Out of the whinnying green stable
          On to the fields of praise.

And honoured among foxes and pheasants by the gay
          house
Under the new made clouds and happy as the heart was
          long,
     In the sun born over and over,
          I ran my heedless ways,
          My wishes raced through the house high hay
And nothing I cared, at my sky blue trades, that time
          allows
In all his tuneful turning so few and such morning songs
     Before the children green and golden
          Follow him out of grace,

Nothing I cared, in the lamb white days, that time would
          take me
Up to the swallow thronged loft by the shadow of my
          hand,
     In the moon that is always rising,
          Nor that riding to sleep
          I should hear him fly with the high fields
And wake to the farm forever fled from the childless land.
Oh as I was young and easy in the mercy of his means,
          Time held me green and dying
          Though I sang in my chains like the sea.

Notes

'THE FORCE THAT THROUGH THE GREEN FUSE DRIVES
THE FLOWER'
This poem and the following one, LIGHT BREAKS . . ., ap-
peared in *Eighteen Poems*, published when Thomas was
twenty. By any standards they are remarkable work for an
adolescent. The poet seems extraordinarily aware of his own
voice, and confident in his symbolism.

Thomas's poetry is in many ways more a product of literary
tradition than of a striking originality. In this poem he is
heavily loyal to the iambic pentameters and imagery of the
early Shakespeare—'the crooked rose', 'the lover's tomb', the
worm and the winding-sheet. The subject-matter of Thomas's
early poems is the traditional subject-matter of adolescence:
a tormented immature sexuality, struggling to break the
child's bonds to the mother (perhaps felt in the second and
fourth stanzas of this poem), and a morbid horror of death
and decay, linked by an aura of guilt to the frustrated sexual-
ity. Much of the force of Dylan Thomas's poetry is in its
suggestions of these basic psychological pressures, rather than
in its superficial statements.

In this poem he presents a series of paradoxes, desperately
felt: at the very moment of maturing he is nevertheless ap-
proaching death. The poem is deliberately timeless, in its
cadences and imagery ('fuse' is the only hint of the twentieth
century, though the rhymes have some debt to Wilfred
Owen). It is melodramatic and histrionic, like much ado-
lescent poetry; but Thomas's flamboyant style is unusually
suited to such gestures.

Sexual and religious suggestions mix in a poem which offers little in the way of coherent statement and can be variously interpreted. The poem seems to be about human life and human emotion, especially the secret or inaccessible parts of personality. The imagery of daylight, sea, fruit, the seasons and the soil asserts a kinship between man and his earthly condition. The poem might well be taken as a test piece for disagreements about the degree to which literature must be consistent and comprehensible: some readers feel that the ambiguity of a poem such as this amounts almost to fraud. Fairly certainly the poem is admired mainly for its music: the first verse in particular has a half-archaic Romantic grandeur which may have been welcome to many readers in the conversational 1930's.

IN MEMORY OF ANN JONES

Ann Jones was the poet's aunt, with whom he often stayed in school holidays; the farm, and the uncle and aunt, figure in many of his stories and poems. After the funeral the poet stands in the 'best room' (described in the first story in *Portrait of the Artist as a Young Dog*) which features a pathetic stuffed fox and stale fern; and he remembers being there as a boy. The contrast of the poet's characteristic rhetoric and Ann Jones's humility is present throughout, and leads Thomas into a half-apology (the lines in parentheses).

Some details are obscure (I don't understand 'four, crossing birds') as often in Thomas's poetry, but there is an onward movement about the poem which helps in the understanding. The first half describes the funeral and the poet's grief; the second describes Ann's goodness. The last ten lines show Thomas at his best: bold images kept under the control of a fundamental seriousness. Some readers will find the last few lines exaggerated, but the poem *is* an oration, on a great and traditional theme, and the rhetoric ought not to frighten us off.

It is interesting to study the unobtrusive use of half-rhyme at the ends of most lines: there is an unflashy craftsmanship here, for which Thomas is often not given credit.

THE CONVERSATION OF PRAYER

The rhyme-scheme involves the mid-line 'ending' as well as the true end of each line; the rhyme-pattern is that of chiasmus (*a.b.b.a.*) and the result is a haunting to-and-fro movement. This is appropriate to the theme, which is that of two prayers, apparently different, 'turning' together, meeting in the darkness, with surprising results.

A REFUSAL TO MOURN THE DEATH, BY FIRE, OF A CHILD IN LONDON

The first nine lines go with 'Never': the first sentence says 'Never till doomsday will I grieve for this child's death'. 'Mankind making/Bird, beast and flower/Fathering' are compound adjectives describing 'darkness'. The girl is no less dead, no less settled into the dignity of death, than her ancestors or those who had lived long lives. She is spared any further suffering: whether one believes in immortality or in extinction, either way she will never die again.

This may seem a strange, even tasteless statement; but Thomas is implying his dislike of conventional sentimental poems on the death of children, which can be more genuinely tasteless. There is a tragic grandeur to the girl's death, which he refuses to cheapen: this is caught in the startling phrases 'the mankind of her going', 'a grave truth' (Shakespearean word-play) and 'the stations of the breath' (recalling the Stations of the Cross).

POEM IN OCTOBER

Thomas writes best about his own childhood: here, at the age of thirty, he takes a day off in the fashion of a boy and walks seeing the world again with that freshness recaptured. It is a poem of light, air, colour and an underlying Christian imagery: the lines dart nimbly about, like the poet's imagination:

. . . the sea wet church the size of a snail
With its horns through mist and the castle
Brown as owls . . .

It is one of Thomas's most successful poems, perhaps because there is no forcing of imagery or theme.

THIS SIDE OF THE TRUTH

For his child, the poet writes a personal creed: the things he sees which Llewelyn does not yet see. Life is a complexity of good and evil, more or less predestined: a loving God supervises all without censorious judgment.

ON A WEDDING ANNIVERSARY

A poem from the war, probably based on a bombing incident. Thomas shows his skill in epigram, and in the single telling word: 'the *wrong* rain'—the word is simple and strong, and the alliteration recalls the saying which is here contradicted—'right as rain'.

THE HUNCHBACK IN THE PARK

Thomas's poetry is mischievous ('Slept at night in a dog kennel/But nobody chained him up') but compassionate underneath (there was nobody to 'chain up' the hunchback, nobody for him to go home to). The hunchback's ideal fantasy could so easily be mocked: but it is presented with kindness and even with respect:

without fault
Straight as a young elm
Straight and tall from his crooked bones

Perhaps the hunchback may conceive a more superb ideal than an ordinary dreamer.

IN MY CRAFT OR SULLEN ART

A poet's statement, slightly sentimentalized; and a musical piece, owing perhaps something to Auden.

AMONG THOSE KILLED IN THE DAWN RAID WAS A
MAN AGED A HUNDRED

The poem is a variation of sonnet-form. The length and
solidity of the man's life is more impressive than the fact of
his death in the air raid. He is too big for the squalor of
warfare. For each year of his life the poet sees a child being
born. Is the nursery-image of the stork as the bringer of
babies successful here?

FERN HILL

A celebration of farm holidays in childhood (see note above
on IN MEMORY OF ANN JONES). Time is benevolent for only
a few years, to the very young: he allows them 'heydays' and
'mercy' and 'morning songs'. But before long all must pass
into the depression of adulthood and oncoming age. Maturity,
sobriety, rational profundity, have no appeal at all for
Thomas; but against this lack must be set the freshness of the
excitement caught in his recollections of childhood and re-
flected in the brilliant coining of phrases: 'the rivers of the
windfall light' . . . 'All the sun long it was running, it was
lovely' (the Welsh voice lies behind this phrasing), 'the horses
flashing into the dark', 'the birth of the simple light' . . .

The last lines of the poem can be clearly linked to the first
poem in this selection, 'THE FORCE THAT THROUGH THE
GREEN FUSE DRIVES THE FLOWER'.

FERN HILL, widely felt to be Thomas's best poem, is a
remarkable mid-twentieth-century throwback to a confident
Romantic ardour we associate with Blake, Wordsworth or the
seventeenth-century poets Vaughan and Traherne. All these
writers see childhood as essentially holier than adulthood, its
amorality as sanctified innocence: images of heaven, Eden,
'the birth of the simple light' characterize their poetry.
Thomas himself is in certain respects a throwback.

Robert Lowell

Robert Lowell was born in Boston in 1917. Lowell is the most famous of the aristocratic Bostonian surnames, and the poet has various influential ancestors. His family represents particularly clearly the now dated Europeanism of New England, and much of his poetry is concerned with a sense of decadence and of an aristocratic tradition he is not at all proud of. Lowell studied at Harvard and Kenyon College; graduated, married, and was converted to Roman Catholicism, all in the year 1940; and in 1943 was imprisoned for conscientious refusal to fight in the Second World War. In 1944 he published his first book of poems, and soon after the war he acquired an international reputation, which increased still more rapidly on the publication in 1959 of *Life Studies*. He has done a good deal of translation and enjoys part-time university teaching.

Lowell's earlier work was an attempt to revive and rediscover the great styles of poetry of the past: it carries more weight the more one knows of Milton, the seventeenth-century Metaphysical poets, and the nineteenth-century French Symbolists, and it derives in manner considerably from the English Victorian Gerard Manley Hopkins (the word 'hurdling' in line 7 of THE QUAKER GRAVEYARD AT NANTUCKET gives the game away in this respect). It is skilful, ingenious poetry, but is often guilty, to my mind, of forcing its effects (the faint suggestion of Dylan Thomas in THE QUAKER GRAVEYARD is disconcerting) and of relying too heavily upon explicit religious doctrine to solve problems which must really be solved by artistic means. There is also a tendency to scholarly erudition for its own sake, characteristic of young academics in the 1930's and 1940's.

The later sequence of poems called *Life Studies*, of which about a third is printed in this selection, seems to me to be much more original and lasting. The elderly cynic might say this is because they were first conceived as prose, because they avoid many of the challenges of conventional poetic rhetoric, and because they are poems of disorientation, fragmentation and psychological defeat. 'What you call today good poetry is what we used to call bad.' But it isn't as simple as that. In the first place, Lowell tells us that after rejecting prose as a means for these purgative reminiscences, because it 'tends to be very diffuse', he then wrote many of them, in the first draft, in strict metre and rhyming couplets. This he found 'stifling', and *Life Studies* emerged finally in fairly free verse; but the remnants of rhyme and metrical discipline are there, and it is remarkable how little looseness one feels in any of these poems. They are also easier poems to understand—Lowell has reacted against his early tendency to put up an impressive intellectual smoke-screen—and, most important, they are courageously honest, earnestly attempting to come to terms with the formative and destructive elements in the poet's own life. The nakedness of statement is often disturbing to the reader, but the instinctive ironic dignity of even the most abject poems carries them well clear of exhibitionism.

'When I finished *Life Studies*,' Lowell wrote in 1960, 'I was left hanging on a question-mark. I am still hanging there. I don't know whether it is a death-rope or a lifeline.' Lowell is unlike the other poets in this book in having quite possibly much of his creative career still ahead of him. If he finds further things to say, it is the technical and artistic discoveries of *Life Studies* which seem most likely to lead him to the means of saying them.

The Quaker Graveyard in Nantucket

(For Warren Winslow, dead at sea)

Let man have dominion over the fishes of the sea and the fowls of the air and the beasts and the whole earth, and every creeping creature that moveth upon the earth.

I

A brackish reach of shoal off Madaket,—
The sea was still breaking violently and night
Had steamed into our North Atlantic Fleet,
When the drowned sailor clutched the drag-net. Light
Flashed from his matted head and marble feet,   5
He grappled at the net
With the coiled, hurdling muscles of his thighs:
The corpse was bloodless, a botch of reds and whites,
Its open staring eyes
Were lustreless dead-lights   10
Or cabin-windows on a stranded hulk
Heavy with sand. We weight the body, close
Its eyes and heave it seaward whence it came,
Where the heel-headed dogfish barks its nose
On Ahab's void and forehead; and the name   15
Is blocked in yellow chalk.
Sailors, who pitch this portent at the sea
Where dreadnoughts shall confess
Its hell-bent deity,
When you are powerless   20
To sand-bag this Atlantic bulwark, faced
By the earth-shaker, green, unwearied, chaste
In his steel scales: ask for no Orphean lute
To pluck life back. The guns of the steeled fleet
Recoil and then repeat   25
The hoarse salute.

II

Whenever winds are moving and their breath
Heaves at the roped-in bulwarks of this pier,
The terns and sea-gulls tremble at your death
30   In these home waters. Sailor, can you hear
The Pequod's sea wings, beating landward, fall
Headlong and break on our Atlantic wall
Off 'Sconset, where the yawing S-boats splash
The bellbuoy, with ballooning spinnakers,
35   As the entangled, screeching mainsheet clears
The blocks: off Madaket, where lubbers lash
The heavy surf and throw their long lead squids
For blue-fish? Sea-gulls blink their heavy lids
Seaward. The winds' wings beat upon the stones,
40   Cousin, and scream for you and the claws rush
At the sea's throat and wring it in the slush
Of this old Quaker graveyard where the bones
Cry out in the long night for the hurt beast
Bobbing by Ahab's whaleboats in the East.

III

45   All you recovered from Poseidon died
With you, my cousin, and the harrowed brine
Is fruitless on the blue beard of the god,
Stretching beyond us to the castles in Spain,
Nantucket's westward haven. To Cape Cod
50   Guns, cradled on the tide,
Blast the eelgrass about a waterclock
Of bilge and backwash, roil the salt and sand
Lashing earth's scaffold, rock
Our warships in the hand
55   Of the great God, where time's contrition blues
Whatever it was these Quaker sailors lost

In the mad scramble of their lives. They died
When time was open-eyed,
Wooden and childish; only bones abide
There, in the nowhere, where their boats were tossed   60
Sky-high, where mariners had fabled news
Of IS, the whited monster. What it cost
Them is their secret. In the sperm-whale's slick
I see the Quakers drown and hear their cry:
'If God himself had not been on our side,   65
If God himself had not been on our side,
When the Atlantic rose against us, why,
Then it had swallowed us up quick.'

IV

This is the end of the whaleroad and the whale
Who spewed Nantucket bones on the thrashed swell   70
And stirred the troubled waters to whirlpools
To send the Pequod packing off to hell:
This is the end of them, three-quarters fools,
Snatching at straws to sail
Seaward and seaward on the turntail whale,   75
Spouting out blood and water as it rolls,
Sick as a dog to these Atlantic shoals:
Clamavimus, O depths; Let the sea-gulls wail

For water, for the deep where the high tide
Mutters to its hurt self, mutters and ebbs.   80
Waves wallow in their wash, go out and out,
Leave only the death-rattle of the crabs,
The beach increasing, its enormous snout
Sucking the ocean's side.
This is the end of running on the waves;   85

We are poured out like water. Who will dance
The mast-lashed master of Leviathans
Up from this field of Quakers in their unstoned graves?

V

When the whale's viscera go and the roll
90   Of its corruption overruns this world
Beyond tree-swept Nantucket and Wood's Hole
And Martha's Vineyard, Sailor, will your sword
Whistle and fall and sink into the fat?
In the great ash-pit of Jehoshaphat
95   The bones cry for the blood of the white whale,
The fat flukes arch and whack about its ears,
The death-lance churns into the sanctuary, tears
The gun-blue swingle, heaving like a flail,
And hacks the coiling life out: it works and drags
100   And rips the sperm-whale's midriff into rags,
Gobbets of blubber spill to wind and weather,
Sailor, and gulls go round the stoven timbers
Where the morning stars sing out together
And thunder shakes the white surf and dismembers
105   The red flag hammered in the mast-head. Hide,
Our steel, Jonas Messias, in Thy side.

VI

Our Lady of Walsingham

There once the penitents took off their shoes
And then walked barefoot the remaining mile;
And the small trees, a stream and hedgerows file
110   Slowly along the munching English lane,
Like cows to the old shrine, until you lose
Track of your dragging pain.

The stream flows down under the druid tree,
Shiloah's whirlpools gurgle and make glad
The castle of God. Sailor, you were glad   115
And whistled Sion by that stream. But see:

Our Lady, too small for her canopy,
Sits near the altar. There's no comeliness
At all or charm in that expressionless
Face with its heavy eyelids. As before,   120
This face, for centuries a memory,
Non est species, neque decor,
Expressionless, expresses God: it goes
Past castled Sion. She knows what God knows,
Not Calvary's Cross nor crib at Bethlehem   125
Now, and the world shall come to Walsingham.

VII

The empty winds are creaking and the oak
Splatters and splatters on the cenotaph,
The boughs are trembling and a gaff
Bobs on the untimely stroke   130
Of the greased wash exploding on a shoal-bell
In the old mouth of the Atlantic. It's well;
Atlantic, you are fouled with the blue sailors,
Sea-monsters, upward angel, downward fish;
Unmarried, and corroding, spare of flesh,   135
Mart once of supercilious, wing'd clippers,
Atlantic, where your bell-trap guts its spoil
You could cut the brackish winds with a knife
Here in Nantucket, and cast up the time
When the Lord God formed man from the sea's slime   140
And breathed into his face the breath of life,
And blue-lung'd combers lumbered to the kill.
The Lord survives the rainbow of His will.

123

My Last Afternoon with Uncle
Devereux Winslow

(1922: The Stone Porch of My Grandfather's
Summer House)

I

'I won't go with you. I want to stay with Grandpa!'
That's how I threw cold water
on my Mother and Father's
watery martini pipe dreams at Sunday dinner.
. . . Fontainebleau, Mattapoisett, Puget Sound . . .
Nowhere was anywhere after a summer
at my Grandfather's farm.
Diamond-pointed, athirst and Norman,
its alley of poplars
paraded from Grandmother's rose garden
to a scarey stand of virgin pine,
scrub, and paths forever pioneering.

One afternoon in 1922,
I sat on the stone porch, looking through
screens as black-grained as drifting coal.
Tockytock, tockytock
clumped our Alpine, Edwardian cuckoo clock,
slung with strangled wooden game.
Our farmer was cementing a root-house under the hill.
One of my hands was cool on a pile
of black earth, the other warm
on a pile of lime. All about me
were the works of my Grandfather's hands:
snapshots of his *Liberty Bell* silver mine,
his high school at *Stukkert am Neckar*,

Stogie-brown beams, fools'-gold nuggets,
octagonal red tiles,
sweaty with a secret dank, crummy with ant-stale,
a Rocky Mountain chaise longue,
its legs, shellacked saplings.
A pastel-pale Huckleberry Finn
fished with a broom straw in a basin
hollowed out of millstone.
Like my Grandfather, the décor
was manly, comfortable,
overbearing, disproportioned.

What were those sunflowers? Pumpkins floating shoulder-
    high?
It was the sunset on Sadie and Nellie
bearing pitchers of ice-tea,
oranges, lemons, mint, and peppermints,
and the jug of shandygaff,
which Grandpa made by blending half and half
yeasty, wheezing homemade sarsaparilla with beer.
The farm, entitled *Char-de-sa*
in the Social Register,
was named for my Grandfather's children:
Charlotte, Devereux, and Sarah.
No one had died there in my lifetime . . .
Only Cinder, our Scottie puppy
paralysed from gobbling toads.
I sat mixing black earth and lime.

II

I was five and a half.
My formal pearl grey shorts
had been worn for three minutes.

My perfection was the Olympian
poise of my models in the imperishable autumn
display windows
of Rogers Peet's boys' store below the State House
in Boston. Distorting drops of water
pinpricked my face in the basin's mirror.
I was a stuffed toucan
with a bibulous, multicoloured beak.

III

Up in the air
by the lakeview window in the billiards-room,
lurid in the doldrums of the sunset hour,
my Great Aunt Sarah
was learning *Samson and Delilah*.
She thundered on the keyboard of her dummy piano
with gauze curtains like a boudoir table,
accordionlike yet soundless.
It had been bought to spare the nerves
of my Grandmother,
tone-deaf, quick as a cricket,
now needing a fourth for 'Auction',
and casting a thirsty eye
on Aunt Sarah, risen like the phoenix
from her bed of troublesome snacks and Tauchnitz
        classics.

Forty years earlier,
twenty, auburn headed,
grasshopper notes of genius!
Family gossip says Aunt Sarah
tilted her archaic Athenian nose
and jilted an Astor.

Each morning she practised
on the grand piano at Symphony Hall,
deathlike in the off-season summer—
its naked Greek statues draped with purple
like the saints in Holy Week. . . .
On the recital day, she failed to appear.

IV

I picked with a clean finger nail at the blue anchor
on my sailor blouse washed white as a spinnaker.
What in the world was I wishing?
. . . A sail-coloured horse browsing in the bulrushes . . .
A fluff of the west wind puffing
my blouse, kiting me over our seven chimneys,
troubling the waters. . . .
As small as sapphires were the ponds: Quittacus,
    Snippituit,
and Assawompset, halved by 'the Island',
where my Uncle's duck blind
floated in a barrage of smoke-clouds.
Double-barrelled shotguns
stuck out like bundles of baby crow-bars.
A single sculler in a camouflaged kayak
was quacking to the decoys. . . .

At the cabin between the waters,
the nearest windows were already boarded.
Uncle Devereux was closing camp for the winter.
As if posed for 'the engagement photograph',
he was wearing his severe
war-uniform of a volunteer Canadian officer.
Daylight from the doorway riddled his student posters,
tacked helter-skelter on the walls as raw as a board-walk.

Mr. Punch, a water melon in hockey tights,
was tossing off a decanter of Scotch.
La Belle France in a red, white and blue toga
was accepting the arm of her 'protector',
the ingenu and porcine Edward VII.
The pre-war music hall belles
had goose necks, glorious signatures, beauty-moles,
and coils of hair like rooster tails.
The finest poster was two or three young men in khaki
    kilts
being bushwhacked on the veldt—
They were almost life-size. . . .

My Uncle was dying at twenty-nine.
'You are behaving like children,'
said my Grandfather,
when my Uncle and Aunt left their three baby daughters,
and sailed for Europe on a last honeymoon . . .
I cowered in terror.
I wasn't a child at all—
unseen and all-seeing, I was Agrippina
in the Golden House of Nero. . . .
Near me was the white measuring-door
my Grandfather had pencilled with my Uncle's heights.
In 1911, he had stopped growing at just six feet.
While I sat on the tiles,
and dug at the anchor on my sailor blouse,
Uncle Devereux stood behind me.
He was as brushed as Bayard, our riding horse.
His face was putty.
His blue coat and white trousers
grew sharper and straighter.
His coat was a blue jay's tail,
his trousers were solid cream from the top of the bottle.

He was animated, hierarchical,
like a ginger snap man in a clothes-press.
He was dying of the incurable Hodgkin's disease. . . .
My hands were warm, then cool, on the piles
of earth and lime,
a black pile and a white pile. . . .
Come winter,
Uncle Devereux would blend to the one colour.

Terminal Days at Beverly Farms

At Beverly Farms, a portly, uncomfortable boulder
bulked in the garden's centre—
an irregular Japanese touch.
After his Bourbon 'old fashioned,' Father,
bronzed, breezy, a shade too ruddy,
swayed as if on deck-duty
under his six pointed star-lantern—
last July's birthday present.
He smiled his oval Lowell smile,
he wore his cream gabardine dinner-jacket,
and indigo cummerbund.
His head was efficient and hairless,
his newly dieted figure was vitally trim.

Father and Mother moved to Beverly Farms
to be a two minute walk from the station,
half an hour by train from the Boston doctors.
They had no sea-view,
but sky-blue tracks of the commuters' railroad shone
like a double-barrelled shotgun
through the scarlet late August sumac,
multiplying like cancer
at their garden's border.

Father had had two coronaries.
He still treasured underhand economies,
but his best friend was his little black *Chevie*,
garaged like a sacrificial steer
with gilded hooves,
yet sensationally sober,
and with less side than an old dancing pump.

The local dealer, a 'buccaneer',
had been bribed a 'king's ransom'
to quickly deliver a car without chrome.

Each morning at eight-thirty,
inattentive and beaming,
loaded with his 'calc' and 'trig' books,
his clipper ship statistics,
and his ivory slide-rule,
Father stole off with the *Chevie*
to loaf in the Maritime Museum at Salem.
He called the curator
'the commander of the Swiss Navy.'

Father's death was abrupt and unprotesting.
His vision was still twenty-twenty.
After a morning of anxious, repetitive smiling,
his last words to Mother were:
'I feel awful.'

For Sale

Poor sheepish plaything,
organized with prodigal animosity,
lived in just a year—
my Father's cottage at Beverly Farms
was on the market the month he died.
Empty, open, intimate,
its town-house furniture
had an on tiptoe air
of waiting for the mover
on the heels of the undertaker.
Ready, afraid
of living alone till eighty,
Mother mooned in a window,
as if she had stayed on a train
one stop past her destination.

Waking in the Blue

The night attendant, a B.U. sophomore,
rouses from the mare's nest of his drowsy head
propped on *The Meaning of Meaning*.
He catwalks down our corridor.
Azure day
makes my agonized blue window bleaker.
Crows maunder on the petrified fairway.
Absence! My heart grows tense
as though a harpoon were sparring for the kill.
(This is the house for the 'mentally ill').

What use is my sense of humour?
I grin at 'Stanley', now sunk in his sixties,
once a Harvard all-American fullback,
(if such were possible!)
still hoarding the build of a boy in his twenties,
as he soaks, a ramrod
with the muscle of a seal
in his long tub,
vaguely urinous from the Victorian plumbing.
A kingly granite profile in a crimson golf-cap,
worn all day, all night,
he thinks only of his figure,
of slimming on sherbet and ginger ale—
more cut off from words than a seal.

This is the way day breaks in Bowditch Hall at McLean's;
the hooded night lights bring out 'Bobbie',
Porcellian '29,
a replica of Louis XVI
without the wig—

133

redolent and roly-poly as a sperm whale,
as he swashbuckles about in his birthday suit
and horses at chairs.

These victorious figures of bravado ossified young.

In between the limits of day,
hours and hours go by under the crew haircuts
and slightly too little nonsensical bachelor twinkle
of the Roman Catholic attendants.
(There are no Mayflower
screwballs in the Catholic Church.)

After a hearty New England breakfast,
I weigh two hundred pounds
this morning. Cock of the walk,
I strut in my turtle-necked French Sailor's jersey
before the metal shaving mirrors,
and see the shaky future grow familiar
in the pinched, indigenous faces
of these thoroughbred mental cases,
twice my age and half my weight.
We are all old-timers,
each of us holds a locked razor.

Skunk Hour

(*For Elizabeth Bishop*)

Nautilus Island's hermit
heiress still lives through winter in her Spartan cottage;
her sheep still graze above the sea.
Her son's a bishop. Her farmer
is first selectman in our village,
she's in her dotage.

Thirsting for
the hierarchic privacy
of Queen Victoria's century,
she buys up all
the eyesores facing her shore,
and lets them fall.

The season's ill—
we've lost our summer millionaire,
who seemed to leap from an L. L. Bean
catalogue. His nine-knot yawl
was auctioned off to lobstermen.
A red fox stain covers Blue Hill.

And now our fairy
decorator brightens his shop for fall,
his fishnet's filled with orange cork,
orange, his cobbler's bench and awl,
there is no money in his work,
he'd rather marry.

One dark night,
my Tudor Ford climbed the hill's skull,
I watched for love-cars. Lights turned down,
they lay together, hull to hull,
where the graveyard shelves on the town. . . .
My mind's not right.

A car radio bleats,
'Love, O careless Love . . .' I hear
my ill-spirit sob in each blood cell,
as if my hand were at its throat. . . .
I myself am hell,
nobody's here—

only skunks, that search
in the moonlight for a bite to eat.
They march on their soles up Main Street:
white stripes, moonstruck eyes' red fire
under the chalk-dry and spar spire
of the Trinitarian Church.

I can stand on top
of our back steps and breathe the rich air—
a mother skunk with her column of kittens swills the
    garbage pail.
She jabs her wedge-head in a cup
of sour cream, drops her ostrich tail,
and will not scare.

The Old Flame

My old flame, my wife!
Remember our lists of birds?
One morning last summer, I drove
by our house in Maine. It was still
on top of its hill—

now a red ear of Indian maize
was splashed on the door;
Old Glory with thirteen stars
hung on a pole; the clapboard
was old-red-schoolhouse-red.

Inside, a new landlord,
a new wife, a new broom!
Atlantic seaboard antique shop
pewter and plunder
shone in each room.

A new frontier!
No running next door
now to phone the sheriff
for his taxi to Bath
and the State Liquor Store!

No one saw your ghostly
imaginary lover
stare through the window,
and tighten
the scarf at his throat.

Health to the new people,
health to their flag, to their old
restored house on the hill!
Everything had been swept bare,
furnished, garnished and aired.

Everything's changed for the best—
how quivering and fierce we were,
there snowbound together,
simmering like wasps
in our tent of books!

Poor ghost, old love, speak
with your old voice
of flaming insight
that kept us awake all night.
In one bed and apart,

we heard the plow
groaning up hill—
a red light, then a blue,
as it tossed off the snow
to the side of the road.

Night Sweat

Work-table, litter, books and standing lamp,
plain things, my stalled equipment, the old broom—
but I am living in a tidied room,
for ten nights now I've felt the creeping damp
float over my pajamas' wilted white. . . .
Sweet salt embalms me and my head is wet,
everything streams and tells me this is right;
my life's fever is soaking in night sweat—
one life, one writing! But the downward glide
and bias of existing wrings us dry—
always inside me is the child who died,
always inside me is his will to die—
one universe, one body . . . in this urn
the animal night sweats of the spirit burn.

Behind me! You! Again I feel the light
lighten my leaded eyelids, while the grey
skulled horses whinny for the soot of night.
I dabble in the dapple of the day,
a heap of wet clothes, seamy, shivering,
I see my flesh and bedding washed with light,
my child exploding into dynamite,
my wife . . . your lightness alters everything,
and tears the black web from the spider's sack,
as your heart hops and flutters like a hare.
Poor turtle, tortoise, if I cannot clear
the surface of these troubled waters here,
absolve me, help me, Dear Heart, as you bear
this world's dead weight and cycle on your back.

Notes

In writing these notes I have made considerable use of *Robert Lowell: The First Twenty Years* by Hugh B. Staples.

THE QUAKER GRAVEYARD IN NANTUCKET

Warren Winslow was Lowell's cousin, lost at sea during the Second World War. The poem is an elegy, consciously reminiscent of the great literary elegies of the past, and especially of Milton's *Lycidas*.

Nantucket was the major base of American whaling activities in the nineteenth century, as described in Herman Melville's novel *Moby Dick*. The poem is full of echoes of this novel, and also of the writings of Henry David Thoreau, another nineteenth-century New England writer.

The Quakers dominated Nantucket and whaling, and whatever their religious theories they sold their souls (lines 56, 62–3) in greedy commercial 'scramble' (line 57)—or so the poet feels. The analogy with twentieth-century American capitalists, the society for whom and by whom Warren Winslow died, is easy to draw. The poem moves through deep grief and moral indignation to a conclusion based on prayer and trust.

Let man have dominion . . . etc.: from Genesis. Its use is ironic: the grasping of the whaling Quakers was something more than mere 'dominion'.

I. The body of a sailor is found, and committed again to the sea. The sea is where man's ancestors (in evolutionary terms) originally came from (line 13): the act of throwing the body back is seen as a vain attempt to placate the mighty god of the sea.

19. *hell-bent*: suggests a malevolence in the sea's destructive power.

22. *earth-shaker*: Poseidon, Greek god of the sea.

140

23–4. Orpheus, the lute-player and singer, according to Greek mythology went to the underworld in an attempt to rescue his wife Eurydice.

24–6. The guns sound over the sailor's body: a salute not only to the sailor but also to the invincible (line 20) might of the sea, against which emotions must be 'steeled' (line 24).

II. A more personal lament for the dead cousin.

31. *Pequod*: the ship in *Moby Dick*.

43–4. *Ahab* was the crazed captain who hunted down the whale Moby Dick; 'the hurt beast' presumably is the whale, on which the Quakers who lie in the graveyard used to prey. There is a subdued, half-suppressed Christian suggestion: bones crying out for one who has been hurt, in the East (the capital letter suggests a doctrinal significance).

III. This section opens by bleakly asserting that nothing which the dead man originally brought from the sea (see note to section I) has survived. The guns boom over savage sea which carries no 'fruit' of the lives it has taken. The poet then turns to the Quakers of the past, to attack their lives (though time—line 55—is to some extent merciful, by gradually disguising—*blues* is a verb—the full horror of their lives). What they lost 'in the mad scramble of their lives' was nothing less than the favour of God, which they were so sure of keeping; in the very moment of drowning (a metaphor for moral disaster, though obviously it has literal relevance) they deluded themselves that God was supporting and saving them.

45. See notes on section I and line 22.

49. *westward*: probably a slip for *eastward*.

51. *waterclock*: perhaps a reference to the regularity of tides.

62. Moby Dick was a white whale. IS seems like the I AM of Jehovah in the Old Testament: in slaughtering the whale the Quakers were warring against God (and the words which follow 'What it cost/Them is their secret' have the terseness of awe and horror).

63. *slick*: patch of oil on the water—here perhaps as a result of a whale's having been butchered.

IV. A depressed recapitulation of what has been said so far.
78. *Clamavimus*: we have cried out. . . . Cf. Psalms cxxx, 1: 'Out of the depths have I cried unto thee, O Lord.'
86–8. Nobody can raise Ahab or his like from the grave. Cf. lines 23–4. *Leviathans*: whales, monsters of the deep; *mast-lashed* seems an adjective more appropriate to the heroes Ulysses and Christ: Ahab died lashed to the whale itself.

V. The vileness and corruption of man's commercial and military organization (still symbolized in the whale-slaughter) are brought to a noisy climax: finally the poet prays that Christ will help us.
89–105. A picture of the end of the world: a nightmare in which the dead Quakers (and perhaps—lines 92–3—even Warren Winslow) will be still lusting for the whale's blood and life, and so missing their chances of salvation. Onomatopoeia, assonance and savage aggressive imagery combine to make a climax of sick horror: note the heaving strength and variety of the verse (e.g. in the placing of caesuras).
89. *viscera*: entrails. *go*: either 'are broken open' or 'go bad'.
94. The Last Judgment, according to one tradition, would take place 'in the valley of Jehoshaphat'. *Ash-pit* because the world would end in fire.
96. *flukes*: the whale's tail.
97. *the sanctuary*: note the religious suggestion.
97–9. Cf. *Moby Dick* end of chapter 61. 'Stubb slowly churned his long sharp lance into the fish, and kept it there, carefully churning and churning, as if cautiously seeking to feel after some gold watch that the whale might have swallowed. . . . But that gold watch he sought was the innermost life of the fish.'
98. *swingle* and *flail* mean more or less the same. The whale —*gun-blue* in colour—is lashing about frantically.

102. *stoven timbers*: the whalers too are doomed (as in *Moby Dick*).

105-6. 'Save us, O Christ the Messiah, by your own suffering, from the damnation we have earned by inflicting suffering.' Christ, one of whose sacred wounds was a lance-thrust in the side, is associated with the whale (as has already been faintly implied in lines 43, 62, 97), but also—more grotesquely —with Jonah, who was swallowed by a whale but resurrected. It is an ambitious piece of Metaphysical wit. The comma after *Hide* seems to be unnecessary and is perhaps a mistake.

VI. The poet looks alternatively to the shrine, in England, of Our Lady of Walsingham: a complete contrast to the previous sections. The terrible ocean of sections I and II is replaced by the calm stream symbolizing the holy spirit, 'the waters of Shiloah that go softly'. This ideal pastoral scene might well have been, for the drowned sailor, his vision of heaven. But the words 'But see:' and the line gap suggest a rejection by the poet of such an easy escapist vision. The figure of Our Lady of Walsingham is less comforting and emotionally appealing, it is inscrutable, a blankness. Lowell is writing of a mysticism which goes beyond not only a conventional view of heaven (123-4) but also the usual emphasis on Christ's earthly life (125): like many mysticisms, it is an enigma.

The whole section is based closely upon a description in E. I. Watkin's *Catholic Art and Culture*.

122. *Non est species, neque decor*: cf. lines 118-19: 'There's no comeliness/At all or charm . . .'.

VII. An after-piece and recapitulation.

128. *cenotaph*: presumably in the graveyard.

132-5. Cf. section I.

134. Cf. Milton, *Paradise Lost* I, 462-3.

136. *Mart*: centre of coming and going, activity.

139–41. Cf. line 13 and notes on sections I and III; also Genesis 2, vii.

142. *combers*: breaking waves (Noah's flood: cf. Genesis vii 10–24).

143. An attempt to condense the poem's statement into a final epigram. Cf. Genesis ix 12–25: God set the rainbow after the flood as a sign of a covenant between God and man: 'the waters shall no more become a flood to destroy all flesh'.

MY LAST AFTERNOON WITH UNCLE DEVEREUX WINSLOW

1922: Lowell was born in 1917. He recalls being aware, at the age of five and a half, that his young uncle was a dying man. The family as a whole is seen as a decadent family (Grandfather, Uncle Devereux and Aunt Sarah all attempt to conduct their lives in false nineteenth-century terms) and it seems more decadent when recollected today: Uncle Devereux's death represents their general sickness. The imagery of *earth* and *lime* (earth and fire?—sections II and III seem half-seriously to complete the four elements with imagery of *water* and *air*) is emphasized at the end of section I and repeated at the end of the poem. The whole poem hovers in a very modern, disconcerting way between tragedy and farce, irony and pathos, form and formlessness (Lowell's verse here often threatens to collapse into prose; but does it ever actually do so?). It is a poem that gains steadily with re-reading, as its shape (and the real relevance of most of the apparently trivial details) appears.

Agrippina, Nero's mother, knew everything that went on in Nero's house; she was a silent power behind the throne.

TERMINAL DAYS AT BEVERLEY FARMS

The second of four poems (FOR SALE is the fourth) about Lowell's father: the first described his disastrously clueless career as a naval officer and financial adviser. TERMINAL DAYS describes his retirement and death. The poet seems harsh in his irony—*vitally trim* at the end of the first paragraph, for a man sadly lacking in real vitality: *multiplying like cancer* at the end of the second paragraph—but his concern to write such poems at all is probably his own sense of reluctant identification with his family: the impotence of these characters is echoed in the bewilderment of WAKING IN THE BLUE and

SKUNK HOUR.
The third paragraph sets the stale nineteenth-century attitudes and diction of Lowell's father against the twentieth-century automobile. For a Lowell, the car must be without 'side' (swagger), a car 'without chrome', 'sensationally sober'.

'calc' and 'trig' books: Calculus and Trigonometry books for Commander Lowell's supposed navigational calculations. The word *loaf* ruthlessly destroys the pretence.

twenty-twenty vision is virtually perfect vision. There is great pathos in this line (one imagines it as a frequent boast of the Commander in his last days) and the next.

WAKING IN THE BLUE
This and the next poem deal with a period of mental illness. Here Lowell is in McLean's, a private mental hospital: the night-attendant is an undergraduate at Boston University, where Lowell himself teaches. *'Stanley'* and *'Bobbie'* are other and probably more permanent inmates of the hospital.

The vivid, fragmentary, basically puzzled consciousness of the mentally disturbed is superbly re-created in this poem. The early imagery is of listlessness ('the mare's nest of his drowsy head', 'crows maunder') and violent anguish ('agonized', 'petrified', 'tense/as though a harpoon were sparring for the kill'; the latter image is taken up painfully in the description of 'Bobbie' who in his youth belonged to the *Porcellian*, the most exclusive club at Harvard). The rhyme at 'This is the house for the mentally ill' jingles in a bitter sick humour, which is in turn the subject of a bitter comment.

The last section is more coherent and sober, but also more

profoundly frightened: the poet sees himself as potentially a permanent 'mental case', like 'Stanley' and 'Bobbie'.

SKUNK HOUR

Elizabeth Bishop is a modern American poet much admired by Lowell. The scene of the poem is Castine, Maine, where the poet has a summer home. The first four stanzas describe local eccentrics, representative of the decaying New England tradition (compare the Uncle Devereux poem). The last four are personal, describing the poet's mental illness with rare honesty and cuttingness. He watches the evidence of lovers, and associates them with death: the hill's skull, the graveyard. He is trapped in himself, the knowledge of his own sickness. The poem ends with a physical image of skunks, the ostracized, traditionally mocked creatures to whom rottenness is natural and not horrific.

MY OLD FLAME

This and the following poem are from *For the Union Dead*, Lowell's latest volume.

Lowell has been twice married; this clear, controlled poem would seem to be addressed to his first wife.

NIGHT SWEAT

The earlier and later Lowell methods meet: this poem combines the apparent casualness and spontaneity of the *Life Studies* sequence with the rhymed iambic pentameters and traditional literary overtones of earlier work. The poem sums up much of the emotional material of the *Life Studies* sequence: self-obsession to the point of horror, self-dramatization, self-pity and ultimate self-abasement (the last lines). The way to sanity and stability for the man too much caught up in himself—his childhood past, his death to come—is through another human being (his wife?), or possibly through the guidance of Christ (who seems to be suggested in the last lines).

ACKNOWLEDGEMENTS

Acknowledgements are due to the following for permission to publish copyright material: Faber & Faber Ltd. for the poems by W. H. Auden from *Collected Shorter Poems 1927–1957*; Curtis Brown, London, for part of 'Letter to Lord Byron' by W. H. Auden; Faber & Faber Ltd. for the poems by Louis MacNeice from *The Collected Poems of Louis MacNeice* and *Visitations*; Faber & Faber Ltd. for the poems by Theodore Roethke from *The Collected Poems of Theodore Roethke*; J. M. Dent & Sons Ltd. and the Trustees for the Copyrights of the late Dylan Thomas for the poems by Dylan Thomas; Faber & Faber Ltd. for the poems by Robert Lowell from *Poems 1938–1949*, *Life Studies* and *For the Union Dead*.

In the case of certain poems, acknowledgements to include them in this collection for use in Canada are made to: Curtis Brown Ltd., New York, for part of 'Letter to Lord Byron', by W. H. Auden, copyright © 1937–65 by W. H. Auden; Doubleday & Company, Inc. for poems by Theodore Roethke as follows—'Idyll' copyright 1939 by Theodore Roethke—'Child on Top of a Greenhouse' copyright 1946 by Editorial Publications, Inc.—'A Field of Light' copyright 1948 by The Tiger's Eye—'Four for Sir John Davies', 'The Dance' copyright 1952 by The Atlantic Monthly Company—'The Partner' copyright 1952 by Theodore Roethke, and 'The Wraith' and 'The Vigil' copyright 1953 by Theodore Roethke—'Meditation at Oyster River' and 'The Sequel' copyright © 1960 by Beatrice Roethke as Ad-